The Diary of Petr Ginz

durch ein warmes Mittagessen.
Meldet Euch
bei dem zuständigen
Magistratamt.
Niemand darf hungern
Nikdo nesmí
hladověti
jedním teplým obědem.
Hlaste se u Vaší místní
magistrátní úřadovny.

The Diary of Petr Ginz
1941–1942

Edited by Chava Pressburger

Translated from the Czech by Elena Lappin

 Atlantic Books
London

Original Czech edition published as *Denik Meho Bratra* by Trigon Publishers, Prague, 2004.

First published in English in the United States of America in 2007 by Grove Atlantic Ltd.

First published in Great Britain in 2007 by Atlantic Books, an imprint of Grove Atlantic Ltd.

Copyright © 2004 by Chava Pressburger

Translation Copyright © 2007 by Elena Lappin

Illustrations and photographs: copyright © 2004 by Chava Pressburger.
Drawings by Petr Ginz: Gift of Otto Ginz, Haifa and from the collection of the Yad Vashem Art Museum, Jerusalem.
The translator wishes to thank David Curzon for his help translating Petr Ginz's poem "Remembering Prague" and the poem that appears on page 59.

1 3 5 7 9 8 6 4 2

A CIP catalogue record for this book is available from the British Library.

Hardback edition
ISBN: 978 1 84354 553 8

Paperback edition
ISBN: 978 1 84354 554 5

Printed in China

Atlantic Books
An imprint of Grove Atlantic Ltd
Ormond House
26–27 Boswell Street
London WC1N 3JZ

Contents

What We Say We Are
Jonathan Safran Foer

Petr Ginz's parents met at an Esperanto conference. That detail jumped out at me from the introduction to Petr's diary, written by his sister, Chava Pressburger. A failed language—a bad idea born out of a good instinct—Esperanto held the promise of universal communication. Everyone would understand everyone all the time: a new Eden would grow out of the rubble of Babel. Petr was, quite literally, the product of that dream.

How much suffering is due to not having the right word? Foreign words are unknown, familiar words are misunderstood or misinterpreted. Words are perverted by our histories (personal and global), by context and tone of voice. Words are bad approximations. There is evil in the world. Evil took young Petr from his parents and shuffled him into the gas chambers of Auschwitz. But evil is not the only thing to fear or struggle against.

I read Petr's diary as the grandson of survivors, as a first-generation American, as a Jew, and as a writer. Unexpectedly, it was this last identity that most informed my experience. While the diary in your hands is a resoundingly *good* book—by just about every imaginable definition—what it stands in opposition to isn't evil, but speechlessness.

*   *   *

Giving a word to a thing is to give it life. "Let there be light," God said, "and there was light." No magic. No raised hands and thunder. The *articulation* made it possible. It is the most powerful of all Jewish ideas: words are generative. Jews are people *of the book*: their parents are words.

It's the same with marriage. You say "I do" and you do. What is it, *really*, to be married? To be married is to say you are married. To say it not only in front of your spouse, but in front of your community, and in front of God. I don't believe in God, but I believe in saying things to God. I believe in prayer. Or I believe in saying aloud what you would pray for if you believed in God. Saying it brings it into an existence that it didn't have in silence.

I once read an essay by a linguist about the continued creation of modern Hebrew. Until the mid-1970s, he wrote, there wasn't a word for frustrated. And so until the mid-seventies, no Hebrew speaker experienced frustration. Should his wife turn to him in the car and ask why he'd fallen so quiet, he would search his incomplete dictionary of emotions and say, "I'm upset." Or, "I'm annoyed." Or, "I'm irritated." This might have been, itself, merely frustrating, were it not for the problem of our words being self-fulfilling prophecies: we become what we say we are. The man in the car says he is upset, annoyed, or irritated and becomes upset, annoyed, or irritated.

Exactly a year ago today, my first child was born. After much debate—the single word was the most difficult piece of writing I have ever done—we named him Sasha, after his grandmother. He is not only identified as Sasha, he *is* Sasha. My son would not exist with another name.

To name the unnamed. To bring the unnamed into existence. There are writers who hold mirrors to the world. "This is what it's really like," they say. "Exactly what it's like. Down to the most exacting detail." That's fine. Such books are often nice to read, and at their best can give us clear and focused pictures of ourselves. But there's something more to which writing can aspire.

I'm not a religious person, but writing for me is religious in this sense: to write is to participate in the creation that began with that first naming, and will continue until someone or something finds an adequate word for "end." To write is to bring into being things whose existences depend on their articulation. Our emotional dictionaries are incomplete, and so are our historical dictionaries, and ideological dictionaries, and our dictionaries of physical experiences, and memories, hopes, and regrets. The dictionaries of our lives are more empty than full. And so our lives are more empty than full. Until we have the words, we cannot be what we really are.

The most powerful passage of Petr's diary comes when he receives notification of his imminent transport to Theresienstadt concentration camp. His specificity, his unwillingness to become sentimental—the passage was written from memory in Theresienstadt—is overwhelming. But even more powerful, to me—maybe because I am a Jew, maybe because I am a novelist, or new father—is the simple fact of a fourteen-year-old writing in such a place. Surrounded by death, and facing his own, Petr put words on paper. Given his unprecedented situation, his words were unprecedented. He was creating new language. He was creating life.

It can be dangerous to treat a diary like this as literature—to find beauty in it, and symbolism, and structure. But how can one not? Here is the beginning of the passage in which Petr recounts learning that he would soon be parted from his family:

Don't think that cleaning a typewriter is easy. There is cleaning and there is "cleaning." If you want the typewriter to shine on the inside and on the out-

side, you have to remove the carriage and wipe the most invisible corners with a small brush. Then you have to use a blowpipe to clear it out. The most difficult part are the spaces between the typebars.

When Adorno speculated about the possibility of literature after the Holocaust, he wasn't asking something about art (as is commonly misunderstood), but about language itself. What meaning can words have in the light of such destruction? Can "loss" have any use? Can "war"? Can "love," for that matter? Will we ever again be able to find the right word?

The answer is yes—it was built into the question—but language must be reconstructed with an energy greater than that of its destruction. This is what we—as readers, writers, and speakers—do. We participate in *tikkun olam*, the repairing of the world, which began only moments after the world's creation. Adam, the first man, was given the task of gathering the divine light—the *goodness*—that escaped the vessels broken by creation. Young Petr, another first man, had a preternatural knowledge of this. Why else, in the shadow of his death, would he have crafted these words as he did? How else could such an effort have been possible? By repairing the dictionary, he was repairing the world.

The diary in your hands did not save Petr. But it did save us.

Translator's Note

At fourteen, Petr Ginz wrote the equivalent of a captain's log on a sinking ship: daily reports about the weather and accounts of the general situation and everyone's activities. He does not mention feelings of fear, powerlessness, sadness, or pain. But they are heavily present in what is left unsaid. Translation usually means to render, faithfully and convincingly, all the nuances of an author's voice—the words, the tone, the rhythm. In the case of Petr Ginz's diaries, it was equally important to capture, or at least hint at, the grave silence surrounding his brief entries.

But not all his writing in this book is of the same succinct quality. Petr Ginz was an extraordinary boy—artistic, inventive, creative, observant, very mischievous, and witty. He was extremely well informed about what was going on in the world at large and in his own environment, and, like the real writer he might have grown into, from time to time broke out of his concise style and allowed his feelings and opinions to find expression in a poem, story, or essay. There is a long poem about the humiliating Nazi laws Jews were forced to accept, which satirizes in the sharpest manner not only the absurdity of the rules themselves but also the Jews' ability to live with them. There is a heartbreaking poem, written as an adolescent in Theresienstadt, about his feelings for the home and life he has lost in Prague. His articles and stories, written for the magazine he edited in Theresienstadt, reflect a unique ability to transcend the environment of a concentration camp and to focus instead on a rich inner world of spiritual and moral values. Everything he wrote was pointing to a future full of excitement and discovery.

The most difficult passage to translate was his description of the day he found out about his own transport, written in Theresienstadt, from memory. Characteristically, it consists not of an emotional outpouring but mostly of a precise description of the work involved in cleaning typewriters, a job he was doing at the time. As I searched for all the right technical terms and even laughed at the pranks he teased his managers with, I understood and felt the acute necessity to concentrate on mundane reality even as it was crumbling all around him, and under his own feet. But the fourteen-year-old Petr Ginz had no illusions: "So I went home. While walking, I tried to absorb, for the last time, the street noise I would not hear again for a long time (in my opinion; Father and Mother were counting on just a few months)."

As a translator, I felt I was watching this boy grow from a child (whose daily life in Prague went on in places so familiar to me from my own Jewish childhood there, many decades later) into a young man, his writing style changing accordingly. But not his voice, which never wavered in its maturity and astonishing self-control. I hope this translation also captures the man in the boy, the extraordinary man he would have become had he been allowed to live.

—Elena Lappin
London

Petr Ginz (1928–1944), *Moon Landscape,* 1942–1944, pencil on paper, 14.5 × 21 cm; Gift of Otto Ginz, Haifa; Collection of the Yad Vashem Art Museum, Jerusalem.

Introduction
Chava Pressburger

1 They were two small exercise books: one had soft black covers cut out from an old school notebook, the other was bound in stronger cardboard with black and yellow stripes, which had probably been removed from a notepad our parents had once used to write down daily household expenses. Petr had made the two exercise books himself from old paper, and used them as diaries. Things were scarce during the war years, and for Jewish children, a nice new exercise book from a stationery shop was completely out of reach.

But Petr enjoyed making those notebooks, as he enjoyed any opportunity to be creative. He used the hand-bound books not only as diaries, but also for his literary writing, for his manuscripts. In his childish imagination he saw himself as a bookbinder, novelist, publisher, reporter, or scientist. He began writing the diary at the age of thirteen, and stopped shortly before he was deported to Theresienstadt, as a fourteen-year-old. The two diaries published here resurfaced in 2003, sixty years after they were written, under very unusual circumstances.

When the American space shuttle *Columbia* was preparing for its takeoff in 2003, the crew included Ilan Ramon from Israel, whose mother had survived the Auschwitz extermination camp. Ilan wanted to take along into space a symbol of the tragedy of the Holocaust. He turned to the Holocaust Museum in Jerusalem, Yad Vashem, which, aside from many other documents and testaments, stored most of Petr's preserved drawings.

My brother was a very talented, creative, hardworking, and curious boy with very varied interests. He wrote articles, stories, and several short novels, and he also loved to draw and paint. His drawing *Moon Landscape* is evidence of Petr's unusual imagination—and it was this drawing that had been selected by Yad Vashem and by Ilan Ramon to accompany him on his space flight.

The tragic fate of space shuttle *Columbia* shook the world. The shuttle exploded upon reentering Earth's atmosphere on February 1, 2003—what would have been Petr's seventy-fifth birthday. Neither Ilan nor the other crew members survived the exploratory flight. A young life that could have made a vast contribution to the progress of all mankind ended in just one moment. The death of the Israeli astronaut Ilan Ramon reawakened the memory of hundreds of thousands of young people who had also stood at the threshold of lives that had been cut short by the Holocaust. Petr Ginz represents and symbolizes these young people.

In the end, it was this drawing by Petr, carried into space by Ilan Ramon, that brought from darkness into the light of day the pages of Petr's diary, written by him from February 24, 1941, until August 1942. Several weeks after the tragic end of space shuttle *Columbia,* someone from Prague contacted the Yad Vashem Museum and offered to sell six exercise books full of Petr's writings, and his drawings. He found these remnants in an old house in Praha Modrany, which he bought some years ago. Although he threw away most of the junk that had filled that old house, he kept these notebooks and drawings, for some inexplicable reason. He was reminded of his "discovery" when Czech television described, in connection with the tragedy of space shuttle *Columbia,* the fate of Prague boy Petr Ginz. Shortly thereafter, he e-mailed to Israel samples of the texts and drawings he had found.

When I saw them, I felt as if Petr hadn't actually died. It seemed to me that he was alive somewhere in eternity and was letting me know by sending this particular message. The newly found items contained two small diaries where Petr had recorded the events from the years 1941–1942, the period before his deportation to Theresienstadt, while we were all still living together at home in Prague. As soon as I saw the pages of the diary and Petr's drawings, I knew instantly that they were genuine. I recognized my brother's handwriting and I also remembered the events he was describing there. Petr's handwriting gradually changes in the diary pages—it becomes nervous and less legible as the date of his call-up to the transport to Theresienstadt approaches. My own distress grew equally, as I read each new page. Petr does not write explicitly about his fear of the future; nevertheless, his notes reflect the black clouds that were gathering upon him and were soon to engulf him.

Together with the diaries, the find also contained Petr's linocuts, especially illustrations to novels of Jules Verne, who was my brother's favourite author at the time. There was also the first part of one of Petr's novels, two more exercise books containing his articles, and finally a list of all his literary writings.

My husband and I decided to travel to Prague to find the owner of Petr's newly found bequest. I had hoped that I would have a legal right to this inheritance from Petr. But after consulting a lawyer, I was told that I had no legal rights whatsoever, because the house where the items were found had belonged to a new owner for more than three years. However, in the end, I succeeded in obtaining the bequest, so that I now own Petr's two diaries and some linocuts. The remainder has become the property of the Yad Vashem Museum in Jerusalem.

2 Petr's diary is very dear to me, as dear as the happy childhood we shared. Yet it had lasted a short time, ending with the beginning of the persecution of Jews by the Nazis. Until then we had lived as a happy family.

According to Nazi Nuremberg laws, children from mixed marriages, where one partner was a Jew and the other an Aryan, were considered "First Degree Mischlings (mixed-breeds)." This meant that we had to submit to the same laws and restrictions as all other Jews (we wore a yellow star, we were thrown out of public schools, at the end of 1941 the Jewish school was closed too, in street cars we were allowed only in the last car if at all, etc.), with only one exception: we were deported to concentration camps only upon reaching the age of fourteen.

This is why our parents had to give Petr away to the Germans when he turned fourteen in 1942. They waited with horror and tension and hope that the end of the war would come before I was taken away as well. But their hope was for naught, and my time to leave came in 1944, a year before the end of the war. In the end, Father was also deported to Theresienstadt (until then, he had been protected by his Aryan wife, according to Nuremberg laws) and Mother stayed home alone. After the liberation, I returned to Prague with my father.

Petr and I were both born in Prague. Father spoke several languages and worked as a manager of the export department of a textile company. He met our mother at an Esperanto conference. Both our parents were progressive people; they looked after our education and healthy lifestyle. We all took up many sports, skiing and ice skating in the winter, swimming and walking in the summer, especially during the holidays.

Mother was from Hradec Kralove; her father was a village teacher. Our frequent visits to relatives in Hradec, especially for Christmas, are among some of my most beautiful memories. Mother loved music; she had a beautiful voice and loved to sing arias to us at home from operas and operettas. This was when we were little. After the war, the Holocaust, and Petr's tragic fate, she never sang again.

Our father was born in Zdanice near Prague; his family came from the Kourim area. Later, they lived in Prague. My grandfather had an antique shop in Jungmanovo Square. Grandfather Ginz was a very educated and wise man. His shop specialized mainly in old, rare books. He was also a talented artist, as witnessed by his small bequest, and he also had literary talents—his business correspondence with clients was often conducted in verse. He died prematurely, at the age of fifty-five, but he took good care of his wife and five children. In the end, everyone from the Jewish side of our family, except for my father, myself, and one cousin, was killed during the Holocaust, so that it could be said that Grandfather's early death saved him from terrible suffering.

I remember our relatives from Hradec and our aunts and uncles in Prague, cousin Pavel Ginz, and Grandmother Ginz, with love and pleasure, but also with pain in my heart.

3 Our parents raised Petr and me to have good manners, discipline, and education. They taught us to distinguish between right and wrong, good and bad.

The Holocaust convinced us that there are evil people in the world, often led by fanaticism, who are capable of murder and merciless torture. But there are also others, those who try to help under any circumstances, and for whom love is all-important. Such people avoid hate, even against the evil they disagree with.

Petr's young spirit was fully directed toward the good. The essence of his interests and desires had its source in the richness of his soul. He belonged to that important category of people endowed with the gift of positive thinking.

My brother wanted to see; not just to glimpse but to really immerse himself in the things he thought about and investigated. He wanted to get to know the essence of the subject of his research and to test the results of his understanding. His great need to perceive things in depth is evidenced by the large number of his drawings that have survived—the Yad Vashem Museum has over 120 of them in storage.

Every child has a number of interests as part of his or her natural development, one of which begins to dominate over time and later determines whether the child becomes a painter, scientist, writer, or leads to some other profession. Petr was interested in almost everything. Today, we can only guess where Petr's life journey would have led and which of the wide spectrum of his interests would have gained preference.

I remember the time when Petr and I were still children. Petr's hair was dark blond, his eyes were serious and blue, but often playfully happy due to some boyish mischief. I remember how during our joint outings Petr walked with his eyes firmly on the ground, and therefore often found some "treasure"— a special veined stone, a bead, or even a coin. I don't remember ever seeing him cry. This would have been beneath his sense of dignity. I, however, cried often and he teased me about it, calling me "sissy missy," which made me cry even more. In 1942 my brother left for Theresienstadt, where we met again two years later: suddenly, Petr had become a tall, thin, and pale young man; his child's face was gone.

From very early youth, Petr was hungry for knowledge. Not even the Nazis succeeded in stifling his desire to learn, when they forced him, like all Jewish children, to leave school. In spite of all obstacles he realized his need for education, almost compulsively. He often planned his activities a month ahead, and then analyzed in detailed summaries how much of what he had intended had been successfully executed. In a report titled "September 1944" we read what he wrote in Theresienstadt before being sent with the transport of September 28, 1944, to Auschwitz, to his death.

May 1944

Eva arrived.[1]

I finished the notes from Ceylon and bound them. Ceylon has been returned. I haven't read all the notes yet, but I did complete the preparatory work for the study of general education: I have read The System of Sociology *by Chalupny, which contains a classification of sciences, and in this framework I have made a plan to learn a little about each science.*

I have read: Gwen Bristow: Deep Summer. *Franck:* Without a Penny Around the World, *the detective novel* The Silky Face, *Chalupny:* The System of Sociology, *Wells:* A Short History of the World, *Pedagogical newsletter, Jiri Valja:* The Storytellers.[2]

I have drawn: The Brewery.

June 1944

I am working in lithography. I have made a physical map of Asia and I have started a world map according to Mercator's projection.

I have read: Otahalova-Popelova: Seneca in Letters, *Arbes:* Crazy Job, My Friend the Murderer, The Devil, *London:* Lost Face, *Musil:* Desert and Oasis, Cosmos, 2 Selections, *H. G. Wells:* Christina Alberta's Father, *part of Descartes'* Discourse on Method.

1. As a child in Prague, Chava Pressburger was called Eva Ginzova.

2. There was an extensive library in Theresienstadt, consisting of books confiscated from new arrivals. Petr had access to it.

I have learned: The Antiquity (Egyptians, Assyrians, Babylonians, Indians, Phoenicians, Israelites, Greeks, Persians, etc.), the geography of Arabia, Holland, and the Moon.

I have drawn: Behind the Lambing Pen and Vrchlabi.

In my head and on paper, I have organized the subject of zoology. I attend evening lectures (on Rembrandt, Mastickar[3]).

I don't visit the cooks any more.

July 1944

I have read: Honoré de Balzac: Eugenie Grandet, *Gorky:* Stories, Fairy Tales and Complaints, *André Theuriet:* The Last Refuge, *Valenta:* Uncle Eskimo.

I have drawn: Behind the Brewery, Buildings.

I am still employed in lithography, but next month I'll work only half a day and take part in the programme for half a day.

I am learning more English. Eleven-twelfths of the map of the world is now traced in ink. I still have to colour it and fill in the towns.

August 1944

I have read: Dickens: A Christmas Carol, *Hloucha:* The Sun Carriage, *Alexander Niklitschek:* Miracles Everywhere, *Flammarion and Schemer:* Is There Life on Stars?, *Lidman:* The House of Old Maids, *Stolba:* From the West of India and Mexico, I, II, *Tomek:* Prague Jewish Tales and Legends, The Science of Man.

September 1944

I have read: Schweitzer: From My Life and Work, *Dinko Simonovic:* The Family Vincic, *Thein de Vries:* Rembrandt, *Thomas Mann:* Mario and the Magician, *Dickens:* A Christmas Carol, *Danes:* The Origins and Extinction of Aborigines

3. Medieval Czech theatre.

10

in Australia and Oceania, *Milli Dandolo:* The Angel Spoke, *K. May:* The Bear Hunter's Son, *Oscar Wilde:* De profundis and other novellas.

Petr left these notes, titled "Plans and Reports," in the Theresienstadt dormitory, where in spite of everything he managed to spend two years full of creative work. They fill me with very sad feelings. Petr's life was cut short the day he was ordered to join the transport to Auschwitz, beginning his painful journey leading to death. They forced him into a cattle car and took him away to a mass grave.

4 The fact that Petr was a boy with a rich imagination is also documented by his literary works and experiments. Between the ages of eight and fourteen he wrote altogether five novels: *From Prague to China, The Wizard from Altay Mountains, Journey to the Centre of the Earth, Around the World in One Second,* and *A Visit from Prehistory.* As these titles suggest, Petr was a great admirer of the French novelist Jules Verne. He was such a dedicated reader of Verne that he wrote one of his novels pretending that Verne was its author: this was *A Visit from Prehistory,* the only of his titles that has survived complete. In its introduction he writes that he found an unknown manuscript in the attic of the house where Verne used to live, and he, Petr Ginz, is presenting it to the reader for the first time.

A Visit from Prehistory is about a huge dinosaur Ka-du, born, as scientists assume, in the depths of an African lake from a prehistoric egg. The monster Ka-du is horrible—it destroys and kills everything in its way—so that in the end it takes over most of the African continent. But it turns out that the prehistoric lizard is in fact a robot, a massive mechanical monster created by a man who wants to use it to control the entire world. Ultimately, the monster is destroyed thanks to the efforts and courage of European scientists Dupont and Baker, and the world is saved.

In a short afterword, Petr (speaking as the writer Jules Verne) formulates a warning that is remarkably topical in view of his own reality:

Belgian Congo was thus freed from a tyrant and the world was liberated from a supposedly prehistoric monster. But it has to be added, is it not possible that a new monster may appear on the surface of this Earth, worse than this one—a monster that, controlled by an evil will and equipped with the most advanced technical means, will torture mankind in a terrible manner? In the progressive nineteenth century it is entirely possible. Who knows?

Several years after writing these sentences, Petr himself became not a symbolic but a real victim of the monster that was Nazism.

5 Petr arrived in Theresienstadt in October 1942, aged fourteen. He stayed there for two years. From all his activities in Theresienstadt it is clear that he believed he would return to the world from which he had been torn, and that he expected to fulfill a certain task in it, a mission for which he had to prepare. He believed that the world was waiting for his contribution.

In Theresienstadt he found out about the horrors that can happen in human history, but it didn't change his direction at all, as illustrated by this quote from an article he wrote there:

They tore us unjustly away from the fertile ground of work, joy, and culture, which was supposed to nourish our youth. They do this for only one purpose—to destroy us not physically, but spiritually and morally. Will they succeed? Never! Deprived of our former sources of culture, we shall create new ones. Separated from the sources of our old happiness, we shall create a new and joyfully radiant life!

These sentences express Petr's spiritual strength, which propelled him even in Theresienstadt to great creativity. Only a small remnant of its expressions has survived.

One of the fruits of his unusual energy was the magazine *Vedem* ("We Lead"), a weekly written by a group of young boys who inhabited House 1 in L 417 in the Theresienstadt ghetto. Petr founded this review, edited it, commissioned articles for it, and if there weren't enough, he wrote them himself under a pseudonym. The magazine *Vedem* published opinion pieces, poems, reflections about the past and the future, thoughts that expressed not only helplessness about the situation at the time, but also faith and hope—often supported by black humour—that it will improve. We find here also poems full of sadness, poems about the world that had been destroyed and demolished. One of these is Petr's poem about Prague, which he loved so much, but which he was never to see again.

Petr Ginz (1928–1944), *Sunflower,* 1944. Watercolour on paper, Gift of Otto Ginz, Haifa; Collection of the Yad Vashem Art Museum, Jerusalem.

REMEMBERING PRAGUE

How long has it already been
since last the sun was seen by me
behind the Petrin hill, dropping out of sight?
I kissed Prague with a teary glance when she
wrapped herself in the shadows of the night.

How long since in Vltava I could hear
the pleasant murmur of the weir?
Long ago the buzz of Wenceslas Square
was forgotten. When did it disappear?

How are those hidden corners of my city
in the shadow of the slaughterhouse? I fear
they are not sad, they don't miss me
as I miss them. It's been a year.

For a year I've been stuck in an ugly hole;
instead of your beauties, I've a few streets alone.
Like a wild animal trapped in a cage
I remember you, my Prague, a fairy tale of stone.

6 This book consists mainly of two diaries written by my brother, Petr. I would like to preface them with a few words. The first one of Petr's diaries contains brief entries about his daily life between September 19, 1941, and February 24, 1942, continuing in the second one from February 24 until August 9, 1942—the time before his transport to Theresienstadt.

It is clear that Petr wrote his journals only for himself and that it never occurred to him that they could be read by someone else. And this is why we find here absolutely truthful accounts about Petr's family life, about his friends and acquaintances, about the environment in which he grew up—and all this at a time when this environment is being destroyed, day after day, by Nazi abuse.

Petr presents all the facts in a dry manner, without expressing emotions, without demonstrating worry, fear, or hate. Thus, the fact that he was thrown off a streetcar because he was a Jew is mentioned next to his report card consisting of all A's.

Petr's diaries are also testimonies of the method used by the Nazis during the Holocaust. Everything appears to be functioning as usual: the Jewish religious community, Jewish hospitals and schools. The Jews' freedom is being restricted only gradually, with new laws being announced with increasing regularity, listing items Jews have to give up, places they are not allowed to frequent, everything they are forbidden to do. More and more people are being called up for transports. Suddenly, a relative is leaving, one pupil or another, or a teacher is missing at school. People help each other pack suitcases for the journey, there is organized assistance for carrying luggage. But those who remain continue to live their seemingly normal lives. A teacher assigns the copying of one hundred nouns as a punishment.

People do not understand. When Mr. Mautner is called up for his transport, he goes to ask at the Jewish Community whether it isn't a mistake. Can this be possible? I am fifty years old, and I have a heart defect! Those who are

16

leaving for Poland have no idea that their carefully packed suitcases are loaded onto a special train car and they will never see them again. They do not suspect that maybe in as little as a week they will be gassed or burned or murdered in some other way.

My brother's diary is written in a calm style, although it changes, together with his handwriting, in the last weeks and days, when he is expecting to be assigned to a transport. His notes are nervous, as if he didn't know what was happening to him and was unable to describe those days. Only in Theresienstadt does he reveal the circumstances of his departure, after the fact, thus completing the diary in which he had not captured this fateful moment.

I am presenting these notes even before the diaries from the years 1941–1942. Although this disturbs the chronology of events, I am of the opinion that it was precisely Petr's assignment to the Theresienstadt transport and his portrayal of the preparations for his departure that throw a light on and a shadow over his earlier diaries, where he writes about his everyday existence in the midst of a threatening situation, but nevertheless pulsating with regular life and without interruption. Incomprehensibly to us today, there was a sense of harmony, and a hope that the future would not bring a tragic end.

I. How I found out about the transport

On the morning of September 22, 1942, I left at seven o'clock, as usual, for my work in 7 Josefovska Street, in a typewriter repair shop. The manager, Mr. Bruck (whom I had nicknamed Wolf), was already there, so was Mr. Fuchs. Mr. Bondy and Mr. Lampl arrived later. The work began immediately after. I cleaned the typewriters and others disassembled them. Don't think that cleaning a typewriter is easy. There is cleaning and there is "cleaning." If you want the typewriter to shine on the inside and on the outside, you have to remove the carriage and wipe the most invisible corners with a small brush. Then you have to use a blowpipe to clear it out.

The most difficult part are the spaces between the typebars. Of course, this varies from one model to another. Cleaning the "Demontable" is no problem at all, you can take it apart completely, but the L. C. Smith is much harder. There, you can only remove the platen.

After I finished cleaning a couple of typewriters (I wrote down the numbers conscientiously. Old Fuchs later copied them and collected payment for the cleaning. Of course, I didn't get paid.), I was sent to inspect typewriters. Every fourteen days there was an inspection of typewriters in all the departments of the Jewish community, to see if any needed cleaning. That day, it was the Legal Department's turn, at 21 Norimberska Street. I was sent there with a small case, in which I carried gasoline for cleaning the platen, alcohol for cleaning the keys, and for the same purpose a wire brush and a cloth. My case also contained several replacement ribbons (13, 14, and 14.5 mm), a notepad for recording the replaced ribbons, a couple of chisels, and an oil can. On the way, I had collected a few cigarette butts. But I found most of them on the stairs of the Jewish religious community center.

I sat down in front of a typewriter in the legal department and began cleaning it. Suddenly, the phone rang. It was the typewriter repair shop, telling me to go to the workshop immediately. I was very surprised, because it was normally I who phoned them (that's when I tore a string somewhere) rather than the other way around. But I kept my surprise to myself, collected my things, and walked to the workshop. As soon as I entered, Wolf said calmly: "You're in it, don't worry about it."

II. Preparations

When Wolf said this memorable sentence to me, I remained surprisingly calm. I said good-bye to them, in case I didn't see them again. I remembered all the mischief I had caused them (for example, I filled the spray for spraying typewriters half with gasoline and half with air, lit a match, placed it in the window, and then blew gasoline fumes into it. The resulting flame was so huge—about three metres long and one metre wide—that it could be seen in the next room. They came running right away, confiscated the matches, and I was told that if I ever did anything like that again, I would get kicked out. This was a case when things turned out well; but another time, while spraying a typewriter, I noticed rings of gas fumes rising in the air, and I wanted to make them burn. I should add that the typewriter was placed in a bowl full of gasoline, with another half of a can next to it. If I had lit those fumes back then, I wouldn't be sitting here writing this.) and I thought they might be pleased I'm leaving. But they looked as if they really were sorry.

So I went home. While walking, I tried to absorb, for the last time, the street noise I would not hear again for a long time (in my opinion; Father and Mother were counting on just a few months). I arrived at home (I hid my star on the way from the corner to the entrance to our building, till I reached the apartment, so that it would not be noticed that Jews still lived in our house). All the way to the third floor there were only offices, on the fourth floor lived the Kohners (they left for Poland three months ago, people say all their luggage was confiscated), the Mautners (they left for Theresienstadt), Ichas (Aryans, railway employees), and us. We had been saved from moving out because the apartment was registered in Mother's name.

Finally, I arrived home and knocked on the door. "Who is it?" Mummy asked from inside. "Me." Mummy opened, surprised that I was home so early. "Mancinka, don't get frightened, I'm in a transport." Mummy was immediately beside herself; she started crying, she didn't know what to do. I comforted her. Suddenly the doorbell rang. Auntie Nada arrived to tell us I was in a transport, but we already knew it. Auntie Nada is a practical soul; she went straight into action. First, we hurried to the community centre to pick up the forms that were about to be distributed. Otherwise we would have heard about the transport only at noon. We were to board at 6 P.M., at Veletrzni Palace. Afterward we ran quickly back home; my good friend, Harry Popper was already waiting to say good-bye to me, which he had succeeded in doing. There was a lot of action; we were packing; some women helpers from the

19

The official letter sent to Petr on October 22, 1942, informing him that he has to report for a transport on the same day. Private archive, Chava Pressburger.

You have been assigned to transport Ca and are ordered to report today, on 22/10/1942, at 6 P.M. at the latest to the assembly grounds Veletrh in Prague VII, entrance opposite Vinarska Street, with all your documents and your hand luggage, which must not exceed the weight of 10kg. Large suitcases will be picked up by our collection service tomorrow morning. Inform the person delivering this letter where these main suitcases will be stored. We are enclosing all the printed information and questionnaires; read through them, fill them out, and bring them with you to the Exhibition Grounds. At the same time we are informing you that you must hand in all food-ration coupons for the next supply period, which you have recently received. We have arranged for our service to help you with your preparations for joining the transport.

Jewish Community arrived to help us pack. In the meantime we somehow managed to eat lunch. I no longer remember what we had for lunch that day, although I would really like to know it; I believe it was hamburgers.

After lunch I was told to choose which of my toys I wanted to take along. I took a supply of paper (including this notebook), linoleum, small knives for cutting it, the unfinished novel The Wizard of Altay Mountains, *which at the time consisted of about 260 pages. I wanted to finish writing it in Theresienstadt, but in the end nothing came of it. I will speak later about laziness in Theresienstadt. I also took thin leather for binding, and a few sheets of endpaper. That was all. Sorry, also a few broken watercolour paints; the rest were left at home. And that was definitely all from my own drawer in the wardrobe, and the big case from Macesky. I packed these items lovingly with the other luggage, and it will probably be seen as bad that I was more worried about losing them than anything else.*

In the middle of the room, on the table the Mautners had hidden with us, there was a huge pile of things that were meant to be packed—the couch and the ottoman were also full. Pavel and Hanka came and helped where possible, and where not. Now that I'm writing this, I'm doing it in a humorous style, but at the time we didn't feel like laughing. Daddy gave me his best shirts and a thick jacket, his ski boots and all sorts of things. I even reminded him jokingly that his own protection wasn't certain. (Protection applied to those married to an Aryan man or woman and their children under the age of fourteen.) At the time, the protection was unreliable. One day you could be protected and the next day deported.

However, we had been prepared for my transport. Because during the last registration in Stresovice, the SS-man said to Daddy about me: "Der fährt mit [dem] nächsten Transport."[4] My parents didn't tell me about it; I just found out about it. I didn't go with the next transport, but the one after.

4. "He is going with the next transport."

III. Departure

The entire afternoon passed away in confusion. My parents were packing my blan-
ket. It was actually a quilted duvet. Auntie Nada was helping with this. I also re-
member Daddy saying: "Let Petr do it, now we are doing it all together but when
he's at Veletrh he'll have to do it by himself." So I took the blanket and packed into
it a few loaves of bread, a pillow, a sheet, and a pair of pajamas. I closed the blanket
and rolled it together by pressing on it with my knees. Then I slipped a sack over it,
which Mummy pulled off the sink. I still remember saying that she won't have any-
thing to cover the sink with. Mummy just waved her hand.

Soon, it was evening. We darkened the room (on other days we rarely did this)
using the ottoman covers. This darkening always involved wild acrobatics. Mummy
used to open the inside window; then she'd stand in the space between both win-
dows and attach the rings on the corners of the blanket to prepared (or sometimes
unprepared) nails or hooks. I was in favor of the closed-window principle. I moved
along the inside window sill and, holding on to the window bolts, darkened the room.
Then I jumped down, making the windows rattle.

We continued packing. Auntie Nada called me into the bedroom and implored
me to be sensible, to stay away from big boys and bad girls.[5] Then she untied the
cuffs on my coat and inside each cuff near the sleeve she put a hundred-mark bill.
In addition, Daddy gave me a kitchen knife with a hollowed-out handle hiding an-
other hundred-mark bill.

We had to do it all quickly, because I had to be there at 6 o'clock. That's why
there were the last feverish preparations. They filled one of my pockets with sausage

5. From here Petr continues to write using a secret code he invented himself but which I succeeded in deciphering. He also uses Cyrilic letters, Hebrew letters (but writes Czech text in
both), and shorthand. In spite of my attempts to decipher the entire coded text a few bits remain illegible: they are marked with three dots […].

sandwiches; my other pockets were also filled with food but now I don't know what they put in there. I'm sure it was something good.

I was to leave at eight o'clock in the evening. We took the tram to Veletrh. This was because Jews who were called up for a transport received a permit for traveling by streetcar from the Jewish Community. You had to show the card and a personal identification document, pay, and only then could you travel. I still remember how Daddy appealed to the other passengers and explained to them how difficult it was. Our transport was in fact the beginning of the Mischling transports. [We] arrived at Veletrh, it was [. . .] dark. Daddy said good-bye to me. He kissed me several times and Auntie Nada gave me the last kiss. [. . .] took [. . .] from the office. I was given a new number, 446. What was actually the name of our transport? They didn't know yet. I handed over my suitcases in the optimistic hope that I would see them again someday.

So this is how Petr described his departure. I am also adding here what our father, Otto Ginz, wrote a few years later about saying good-bye to Petr:

Near the exhibition area there were large sheds, where the victims, selected for transport to Theresienstadt, were told to assemble. The Prague Jewish Community covered the soil with old mattresses. On October 22, 1942, I accompanied our Petr there. We had an earnest talk, but I avoided triggering sad thoughts in him, and we comforted each other by saying that we would both meet at home soon. On the basis of examples I knew I warned Petr in the last moment before his departure to be careful when dealing with German guards, with whom he would soon be confronted. We reached the point beyond which those accompanying the victims were not allowed to go, I pressed our Petr to me, we kissed, and Petr went inside. He turned around a few times, we waved to each other, and Petr disappeared in the gate. I turned away and at that moment a loud cry escaped my insides, more like a scream of pain. I controlled myself and forced myself to calm down. I don't know how I made it home. I was well aware that my wife's nerves would not have managed the separation I had just lived through.

The terrible moments of our parting ended the two-year period recorded in Petr's diaries, which I now present here. These were the last two years Petr had lived with his family and friends, in the environment where his life had begun—and from which he was torn.

Notes by Petr Ginz at Theresienstadt, written in a cryptic code that he invented.
From the private archives of Chava Pressburger.

Editor's Note
Chava Pressburger

Petr Ginz's diaries and other texts have been copied without changes as closely as possible, while adhering to orthographic rules of the time. The diary headings have been given a unified form, according to the one used most frequently by Petr in his diaries: the days as Arabic numerals, the months as Roman numerals, followed by the year and in brackets the day of the week. Inconsistencies have been corrected during the copying of the entries. To facilitate the understanding of the text some details referred to as numerals have been rewritten as words, e.g., 4 children—four children. We also detail irregular abbreviations. A small number of grammatical and spelling errors have been corrected. In a few exceptional cases the syntax has also been corrected. Words that have been added are placed in square brackets.

Petr Ginz's Diary

from 19th September
of the year nineteen hundred and forty-one
(Friday)
till 23rd February
of the year nineteen hundred and forty-two
(Monday)

Material donated as a birthday gift by Eva Ginzova.[6]

---

6. Petr used to make and bind his own notebooks for his novels and diaries, because new exercise books from a shop were not available to Jews at that time. This diary was made from old paper I had obtained for him.

19. IX. 1941 (Friday)

The weather is foggy. Jews were told to wear a badge, which looks approximately like this:

When I went to school,[7] I counted sixty-nine "sheriffs," Mummy counted more than a hundred of them.

Dlouha avenue is now called "The Milky Way."

In the afternoon I went with Eva to Troja; we went on a ride on a tethered boat.

20. IX. 1941 (Saturday)

Cold in the morning, nice in the afternoon.

In the morning I had to study. In the afternoon I went (to Troja) with Popper,[8] from whom I bought a tank for 270 crowns. Mummy, Daddy, and Eva were at Grandma's.

7. Petr attended a Jewish school on Jachymova Street; the language of instruction was Czech.

8. Harry Popper, Petr's friend.

28

21. IX. 1941 (Sunday)

Very nice weather all day.

I wrote my homework all morning, in the afternoon till three.

The Miloses[9] will come here around four and we'll go to Troja.

(Eva II[10] arrived as well, and the Blochs, from whom I received photographs.)

22. IX. 1941 (Monday)

In the morning there was a terrible fog, in the afternoon it was nice.

In the morning I went to wish Grandma "Le Shanah Tovah,"[11] then I accompanied her to the Smichov synagogue.

In the afternoon, because it's Rosh Hashanah, we have no school.

We all went for a walk near the slaughterhouse; we rode on rafts until the evening.

23. IX. 1941 (Tuesday)

In the morning there was fog; at noon and in the afternoon it was very nice.

Popper and I went to the slaughterhouse in the morning.

It is the autumn equinox, the beginning of autumn, but I have already seen fallen leaves somewhere.

I spent the afternoon at home.

9. "Miloses" is how we referred to the family of Milos Ginz, an uncle on Father's side. Similarly, we referred to the Jirins, the Miluskas, the grandmas, and so on. Uncle Milos and his wife Nada had a son called Pavel, my and Petr's first cousin.

10. Petr referred to Eva Sklenckova, our cousin on Mother's side whose married name later became Simkova, as Eva II.

11. Wishes for the Jewish New Year.

24. IX. 1941 (Wednesday)

Fog in the morning, afternoon nice.

In the morning in school, in the afternoon with Popper in Troja.

25. IX. 1941 (Thursday)

In the morning chilly, in the afternoon nice.

In the morning in the library, in the afternoon at school.

At Denis train station there was a fire engine; smoke was blowing from there.

Mummy heard a terrible bang, then many smaller ones.

Probably another sabotage.

27. IX. 1941 (Saturday)

Quite nice all day. In the morning at home, in the afternoon with Popper and Martin in Troja. Martin became a member of SPVL, which made Popper very angry, because M. is not allowed to give up a membership that forbids him to sign contracts, without my permission. M. invited me to his house for his birthday. So on Sunday I'll go to him.

I arranged a boycott against Popper.

They announced a so-called civil state of emergency (martial law) valid from 28. IX. 1941, 12 o'clock.

Signed by Heydrich instead of Neurath.

28. IX. 1941 (Sunday)

Nice weather all day, especially in the afternoon.

In the morning I was at home, did my homework; in the afternoon I went to Turna's house for a snack; we also went to the Atlantic, where we tried out ships.

I cancelled the boycott against Popper, who was threatening me with war. I

Petr Ginz (1928–1944), *Ex Libris Harry Popper,* 1941. Linocut; Collection of the Yad Vashem Art Museum, Jerusalem.

made a pact with Martin, according to which I will supply him with ships in case of war.

Then we played Mill (Nine Men's Morris) and checkers.

I am writing this in the evening by candlelight, my parents and Eva II went to the Levituses[12] with spoiled sausages. Now it's almost eight o'clock and they're not back yet. P.S. I gave Turna "Mother Bear Brumka and Her Son" as a present.

The tower clock is striking eight right now.

29. IX. 1941 (Monday)

Morning quite cold, afternoon fair.

I was in school this morning, now I'm at home and soon I'll go to my orthopedic exercise and school exercise class.

I've been to the gym, then wasted time in school, where we were supposed to have handicrafts, and this because of the "Nine-tailed cat with eighteen iron balls" from Bardach.[13]

30. IX. 1941 (Tuesday)

Quite cold all day.

Morning at home, afternoon in school.

12. Our father, Otto Ginz, had four siblings: two brothers, Milos and Slava, and two sisters, Herma and Anda. Aunt Herma married Karl Levitus.

13. Felix Bardach, Petr's classmate.

1. X. 1941 (Wednesday)
It has been raining all day. It is Yom Kippur,[14] I fasted from Tuesday evening until Wednesday evening. But in the evening I ate a lot.
Lots of people were executed for preparing the sabotage, illegal possession of weapons, and so on.

2. X. 1941 (Thursday)
Quite cold. Nothing special.

3. X. 1941 (Friday)
Cold in the morning, decent weather in the afternoon.
In the afternoon I went to my orthopedic exercise class, afterward went for a walk near the slaughterhouse. I met Popper there.
There was terrible shellfire at night and shots in the direction of Letna.
Sirens were wailing like mad. The Turnas were in the shelter. Mummy and Daddy heard the whirring of a motor. But not me. Daddy saw shrapnel bursting into pieces a few times.

4. X. 1941 (Saturday)
Fair weather all day.
In the afternoon I visited the Turnas, and I went to Troja. We were supposed to have a race, but it didn't happen, because some boy (age 14–15) kept throwing stones at us. On the way, Turna was stopped by a small, about eleven-year-old boy, telling him that he shouldn't talk to Jews.

14. The Day of Atonement, a Jewish holiday and fast day.

He also said that he knows the law very well and that he will find out Turna's name.

From Popper I got as two prizes for the boat race a small English textbook. In Troja I met my parents.

5. X. 1941 (Sunday)

In the morning bad fog, in the afternoon quite chilly.

Did homework all morning. In the afternoon we went for a walk in Maniny,[15] where we met the Hirschs; with them we walked far beyond the Liben bridge. I borrowed "The Mysterious Dune."

6. X. 1941 (Monday)

Quite nice weather.

It is Sukkot[16] and so there is no school. In the morning I was at home, in the afternoon at my orthopedic exercise class and I also went to hand in the solution of the competition in "Paradise Garden," where I met a lady who looked more like death than a human being.

15. Maniny was where Petr probably spent most of his free time. It's not a location in Prague Holesovice, as the name would seem to suggest, but dead-end river branches and canals framing Rohansky Island—the word "manina" (from the Czech "chodit mani"—indicated a landscape without roads, which one could criss-cross freely, i.e., however one chose). One of the local canals was filled during the war with city rubbish. Gradually, the river branch and all the canals were filled, so that Rohansky Island is in reality no longer an island.

16. Sukkot is the Feast of Tabernacles, a Jewish holiday commemorating the forty years the Jews spent wandering in the desert during which time they dwelled in huts.

There is a new inventory of Jewish linen, furniture, sewing machines, and other things. The Milos family came to visit us this afternoon (only Uncle and Pavel) and Eva II. Mr. Fried came back recently (he had been arrested by the Gestapo) and immediately got married.

7. X. 1941 (Tuesday)
Weather quite good in the morning, nice in the afternoon.
In the afternoon I was with Eva in Maniny; we rode a trolley cycle.
In the morning I borrowed from Slavek "In a Sailboat across Two Oceans."

8. X. 1941 (Wednesday)
Quite nice weather all day.
In the morning at school, in the afternoon at Maniny. I picked goldenrod there.
In the evening Lianka came to look at Eva's drawings.

9. X. 1941 (Thursday)
Quite nice weather.—Morning at home, afternoon at school, wrote Czech composition essay.

10. X. 1941 (Friday)
In the morning at school, Ehrlich from the parallel class is leaving with the first transport of five thousand Jews to Poland.
Everyone is allowed to take along 50 kg luggage, money, blankets, food, and insurance policies.
In the afternoon (evening) Eva II and Hanka Steiner came to visit.

11. X. 1941 (Saturday)

In the morning I was at home; in the afternoon we visited Grandma. I received a police summons; Eva thought we were already going to Poland. It was about a finder's fee. Because three weeks ago, I found latchkeys, which I handed in to the police. I gave them my address, to send me a finder's reward, in case there was one.

In the evening Eva II was here; she is expecting Otik's arrival.[17]

12. X. 1941 (Sunday)

Finally, after a telephone call and a cable, Otik arrived at about 9 A.M. Uncle Jarka D. is also supposed to come soon.

13. X. 1941 (Monday)

There is no school, because it's Sukkot on Monday and Tuesday.

I received notice to go to school and fill sacks with sawdust. In the morning I filled sixty sacks with a group that also included Pavel G. In the afternoon we stuffed over eighty sacks. They reached the ceiling. Two cars delivered the sawdust. The full sacks are sent to Veletrzni Palace, where Jews are supposed to stay for five days before the journey to Poland. I guess they'll sleep on the sacks. Uncle Jarka D. arrived from Hradec; in the evening he went to Horalka's. Eva II was here, too.

---

17. Ota Sklencka, brother of Eva II, our cousin on Mother's side. Later a well-known Prague actor.

14. X. 1941 (Tuesday)

In the morning I went to the police and to Grandma's. At the police station I received 9.90 crowns for the keys. In the afternoon I went for a walk with Eva at Maniny, where I met Fabian from IV.C.

15. X. 1941 (Wednesday)

In the morning I was in school; Kaufman and Hayek will be leaving for Poland.

In the afternoon I was with Popper at Maniny and near the slaughterhouse. Uncle Jarka D. left in the evening. Eva II is here.

16. X. 1941 (Thursday)

In the morning I went for a walk at Maniny and near the slaughterhouse. At Maniny I was invited to ride on a train, by a railway worker. He chatted with me very nicely, said he was from Sudeten Germany, where he left a house. He asked me whether Daddy couldn't sell him an overcoat, since we have to leave everything to the Germans.

In the afternoon at school, a maths exam.

D. Storzova was here; she is leaving with a new transport for Poland.

17. X. 1941 (Friday)

In the morning I went to school, from where I was sent with three others to help put together desks in a new Jewish school in Vinohrady.

We made it back to school just for the last lesson.

In the afternoon I went for a walk near the slaughterhouse and at Maniny. Auntie Anda visited us.

18. X. 1941 (Saturday)

In the morning I was helping out at home.

I scraped out Daddy's sticker albums and glued in new stickers. I did the same work for part of the afternoon. Uncle Milos and Pavel came. In the evening Lianka came to show us her new dress, which she made herself. Mr. Pokorny came, too.

19. X. 1941 (Sunday)

I spent the morning at home; I started a fire in the stove for the first time by myself, now it's burning like crazy. I stayed home in the afternoon as well, just toward the evening I went with Eva to Maniny.

20. X. 1941 (Monday)

In the morning at school, in the afternoon at Maniny. Pavel came in the evening.

21. X. 1941 (Tuesday)

In the morning at home, in the afternoon at school.

We now have Miss Lauscherova as our class teacher, right away she gave four children after school detentions and five written punishments (5x a certain fairly long article). Promising beginning!

22. X. 1941 (Wednesday)

Morning at school. Uncle Milos came at noon.

Mr. Pitter and Eva II came in the evening.

23. X. 1941 (Thursday)

This morning I was in town; in the afternoon I went for a walk.

24. X. 1941 (Friday)

Morning at home, afternoon [incomplete]

25. X. 1941 (Saturday)

In the morning in town and on a walk. In the afternoon I went to visit Popper; Martin was there, too; we played "Business" and "Bell and Hammer." Afterward I was outdoors.

26. X. 1941 (Sunday)

In the morning at home; in the afternoon I visited the Hanzls with the Miloses. Neither Pavlicek nor Jozka or Jirina was at home. Only Miluska[18] was there, who had a visit from Mr. Karpeles. She showed us sleeping bags.

This year's first snow fell today, of course mixed with rain.

We and the Milos family received a summons to register.

27. X. 1941 (Monday)

Morning in school; in the afternoon went to Zizkov.

We got a big punishment from Miss Lauscherova for talking: to decline twenty-five words in German.

We've already had a proper snowstorm.

28. X. 1941 (Tuesday)

Afternoon in school, morning in town.

---

18. Miluska and Jirina—our father's cousins—married two brothers, Otta and Pavel Hansel. Petr writes about them as "the Jirinas" and "the Miluskas." Both families, including the four-year-old Pavlicek, were assigned to one of the first transports of the year 1941. They were sent to Lodz in Poland, all to be killed.

29. X. 1941 (Wednesday)

Morning in school; I got paid 100 crowns for helping out in school. It's enough! On Friday, the Miluskas and the Jirinas have to report to the exhibition grounds. They are leaving for Poland.

On Sunday they weren't yet registered, on Tuesday they registered, and on Wednesday they were called up (at night, as usual).

In the afternoon we visited the family Levitus; Aunt Anda was there too.

30. X. 1941 (Thursday)

In the morning at the Levituses; they have everything ready for the journey to Poland.—Afternoon in school.

(ON LOOSE LEAF WITH SECRET WRITING)

1. in the afternoon there was
2. at our house one
3. lady from Kotrovice (Kotovice?) near Pilsen
4. and she talked about a big
5. attack by the English. One
6. bomb fell about ten feet
7. from the train station and made
8. there an enormous ditch, which
9. they then had to cover for a long
10. time. That sort of attack
1. happened there three times, but they never
2. hit the train station, which
3. is used to transport goods from

4. the Skoda factory.
5. The noise was so terrible,
6. that they thought they were surrounded by
7. cavalry. There was a large number
8. of aeroplanes
9. about Monday 4.V.42
10. some postmen saw
11. at night during the air attack a huge
12. number of aeroplanes.

31. X. 1941 (Friday)

In the morning I was supposed to go to school, but instead I went to say good-bye to the Miluskas and the Jirinas. I brought little Pavlicek something to play with while traveling: a tank and a monkey that jumped and turned somer-saults, but which scared him terribly. There was an awful mess, they are preparing for the journey. Afterward I went to school. The snow stayed a while on the streets for the first time, the roofs are covered.
Afternoon at home.

1. XI. 1941 (Saturday)

In the morning a walk near the slaughterhouse at Maniny, in the afternoon at Grandma's. It's really freezing already, the Maninsky canal is almost completely frozen, the ice is about 1 cm thick. Of course, you can't yet walk on it. In several places there are ice patches you can slide on.
Daddy was called up for work by the Jewish Community (probably at the exhibition center).

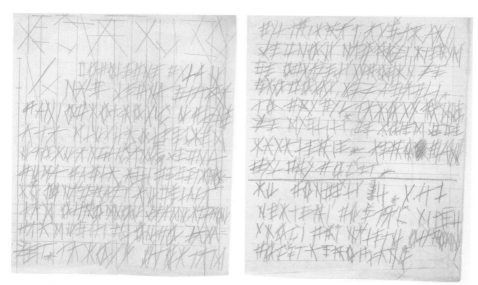

In a self-invented cryptograph, Petr recorded news from the BBC transmitter, which he secretly listened to even though such activity was severely punished.

2. XI. 1941 (Sunday)

In the morning I wrote my homework and my punishment, in the afternoon we were with the Miloses at the Masaryk station, expecting the arrival of Auntie Nada from Budyne. Auntie arrived, and we all went to our house, where we (us children) played "Sorry."

Mr. Pokorny was here in the evening.

3. XI. 1941 (Monday)

School in the morning. We received a letter from the Jewish Community, ordering us to go to Regnart Street and sign that we will not sell or give anything to Aryans. At home in the afternoon.

Daddy worked from 10 till 5 at the exhibition ground. This is the work he had been called up for on Saturday.

4. XI. 1941 (Tuesday)

We have no school till next Monday, probably because people will be going there to sign declarations (see Monday).

I spent the morning at Grandma's where I was working on engravings. Grandma then gave me two. I coloured[19] them in the afternoon.

5. XI. 1941 (Wednesday)

Morning at home, afternoon at the Levituses.

6. IX. 1941 (Thursday)

I spent the morning at Grandma's, where I got more engravings (altogether eighty-three) for colouring. In the afternoon I started on them and finished colouring three of them: Eva also did one.—Went to Maniny in the early evening.

7. XI. 1941 (Friday)

In the morning at home, in the afternoon at Maniny.

8. XI. 1941 (Saturday)

In the morning with Popper near the slaughterhouse and at Maniny, in the afternoon at Grandma's.

9. XI. 1941 (Sunday)

In the morning at home, we have a punishment (from Miss Lauscherova) to decline one hundred nouns with adjectives, so I had to write it. Spent the afternoon with the Milos family.

19. Our grandmother had many old engravings—Grandfather used to own an antique shop—which Petr and I often coloured with watercolours.

10. XI. 1941 (Monday)

In the morning at school, in the afternoon went for a walk.

11. XI. 1941 (Tuesday)

In the morning in town, in the afternoon in school.

12. XI. 1941 (Wednesday)

In the morning in school, in the afternoon with Popper.

The Mautners gave me engravings. Eva II was here.

Aunt Herma gave us a kind of bowl that chirps when the milk is about to spill out. We tried it out today; it works.

13. XI. 1941 (Thursday)

In the morning at the outpatients hospital, in the eye department they gave me a prescription for glasses.

Afternoon in school.

14. XI. 1941 (Friday)

In the morning at school, in the afternoon in town and at Grandma's. We also stopped off at Mr. Repa's on Hybernska Street for those glasses, which we're supposed to receive tomorrow.

15. XI. 1941 (Saturday)

In the morning we borrowed a small heater from the Mautners.

In the afternoon at Grandma's, the Hornsteins (Grandma's tenants) have been called up to report to the exhibition grounds, to go to Poland.

16. XI. 1941 (Sunday)

In the morning at home, in the afternoon at the Levituses; the Milos family was there too. I played chess with Pavel for the first time. Afterward we boys and the girls chased one another through the rooms.

17. XI. 1941 (Monday)

Morning at school, I was tested in natural history and geography (B and A). In the afternoon [incomplete]

18. XI. 1941 (Tuesday)

In the morning at home, in the afternoon at school; I was elected class president.

19. XI. 1941 (Wednesday)

In the morning at school I was publicly named president of class IV.B.
In the afternoon I went to pick up the glasses from Repa's on Hybernska Street and afterward I wore them when I went for a walk with Popper in Troja.

20. XI. 1941 (Thursday)

In the morning at home, in the afternoon at school.
We went to register on Letenska Avenue.

21. XI. 1941 (Friday)

In the morning at school, in the afternoon in Troja.

22. XI. 1941 (Saturday)

In the morning with Popper, in the afternoon at Grandma's, where I received a beautiful inlaid fountain pen.

23. XI. 1941 (Sunday)

In the morning at home, in the afternoon with the Miloses at Maniny.
Transports to Poland (five thousand people have already left in five transports) are stopped for the time being; now they are sending people to work in Theresienstadt.

24. XI. 1941 (Monday)

In the morning in school.
During recess at PE I locked the locker room with a wire with three trainers inside.

25. XI. 1941 (Tuesday)

Morning at home, afternoon in school.

26. XI. 1941 (Wednesday)

In the morning in school, I was called to help people who are going with the new transport to Poland on 27. [XI.]. I waited the entire afternoon just to receive the pass, because Jews are not allowed out on the street before 6 A.M., and I had to be at Mr. Emil Bondy's on Klimentska Street at 5:30 A.M.
I also received a telephone token, so that I can call the Community in case I couldn't carry the luggage.

27. XI. 1941 (Thursday)

Daddy got up at five in the morning and went to those Bondys instead of me. They had a huge amount of luggage and I would definitely not have been able to carry that.—In the afternoon at school, a maths test.

28. XI. 1941 (Friday)

In the morning at school. The Mautners, who live on our floor, have to leave for Theresienstadt, together with thousands of other people. Among others that are leaving is Reach, Ervin Mautner, and many others. Mr. Mautner went to the Community (Jewish) to ask if it wasn't a mistake (he is over fifty years old and ill). In the later afternoon we went for a walk through town over the Charles bridge, Klarov and Belcredi's Avenue (today's Letenska).

The geography teacher Mr. David got married (probably yesterday), so our class bought him a kerosene cooker, Primus. It cost 80 crowns, which amount was collected by our class (IV.B) (in fact we collected 120 crowns; 40 crowns went into the class fund). I wrote a poem to go with it and both were gift-wrapped, but Mr. David was at the registration so we can only give him the present on Monday.

29. XI. (Saturday)

In the morning with Popper near the slaughterhouse, in the afternoon at Grandma's.

Mr. Mautner has already been to the Community; they said it's not an error. So he has leave for the exhibition grounds already on Monday 1.XII. In a month the whole Mautner family will join him.

30. XI. 1941 (Sunday)

In the morning at home, I had to write a punishment (to analyse fifty complex sentences). I spent the entire morning on it.

In the afternoon at the Levitus's; the Milos's and Aunt Anda were there, too. Mr. Mautner came to say good-bye to us. Soon after Mrs. Mautnerova came to get him. They say that from May 1 they've had nothing but trouble. Egon has been arrested, Karel was sent to work in Ceska Lipa, all of their relatives are either in Poland or in Theresienstadt.

1. XII. 1941 (Monday)

In the morning at school, Mr. David accepted that Primus with thanks.

2. XII. 1941 (Tuesday)

Morning at home, afternoon in school. At 11 o'clock the new wooden Pfitzner's bridge was festively opened by the deputy of Mayor Klapka (who was executed).

3. XII. 1941 (Wednesday)

Morning in school. A contest for the class magazine *Outlook* was announced, for the best solution to a certain question that was to be turned into a story. Afternoon at home.

4. XII. 1941 (Thursday)

In the morning I was in town, in the afternoon at home.
They say that transports to Theresienstadt have been stopped at least until January 10.

5. XII. 1941 (Friday)

Morning in school, afternoon at home.

6. XII. 1941 (Saturday)

In the morning I was with Popper near the slaughterhouse, in the afternoon at Martin's, where we played football with coins. I defeated Popper 12 to 1, Martin beat me 4 to 3. I borrowed the Verne books *City of Steel* and *In a Balloon around the World*. (Translator's note: the first book is probably what is known in English as *The Begum's Millions,* and the second could be either *Five Weeks in a Balloon* or *Around the World in 80 Days*—it's not clear which.)

7. XII. 1941 (Sunday)

In the morning at home. The Mautners, now the entire family except for Karl, who is in Lipa, and Egon, who is their nephew, are leaving for Theresienstadt to join Mr. Mautner. Mrs. Mautnerova has been crying a lot; she wants to take Egon along with her. I was at their flat and they gave me all sorts of small things.

8. XII. 1941 (Monday)

In the morning at school. Mr. David has only just managed to read that poem (see 28.XI.) and publicly thanked me for it.
I had gym. I was at home in the afternoon.
Japan has officially declared war against the United States of North America.

9. XII. 1941 (Tuesday)

In the morning I did my homework. The Japanese attacked Singapore.
School in the afternoon.
When, as usual, I walked home from school with Bardach, on Vezenska Street in front of a pub there was a "green anton" (i.e., a van for prisoners) and in front of it stood a line of policemen across the pavement. The Gestapo men then chased some people out of the pub (about eight of them), directly into the "green anton," which they then locked and drove away. I heard it has to do with the geese and chickens displayed in the pub.

10. XII. 1941 (Wednesday)

In the morning I was in school, in the afternoon shopping.
In the evening Eva and I went to say good-bye to Mrs. Mautner and Egon, who volunteered to go to Theresienstadt. They are already leaving tomorrow morning.

We received a nice goose from Hradec, weighing seven kilo (3 kg of lard, 320 g livers).

11. XII. 1941 (Thursday)
The Mautners left in the morning, everyone was crying, they went away like galley-slaves with a number on their coats. Workers from the community (the Jewish religious) carried their luggage.
Karel was supposed to arrive from Lipa, but so far hasn't come.
Mrs. Mautnerova, crying hard, asked us to give him her regards. The apartment keys have to be handed in to the Germans.
Mrs. Mautnerova was having crying attacks.
The hanging Stefanik Bridge (now called the Leos Janacek Bridge) has been closed to pedestrians for quite some time.
In the afternoon at school. Germany declared war on America.
South American states have joined in against Japan (already on Monday the 8th, I heard). Daddy was in the emergency clinic in the afternoon.

12. XII. 1941 (Friday)
In the morning at school. On the way I saw six moving vans, they were moving the equipment from Dusni synagogue; about twenty Jews in working clothes (among them Uncle Milos) were carrying furniture. We had to hand in Eva's ski boots, because the Germans ordered it.
In the afternoon at home. In the evening Daddy was with the emergency service, see 13. XII. 1941.

13. XII. 1941 (Saturday)

Spent the morning with Popper. I bought two books from him (one small German one, the other one *Little Lord*). Karel Mautner arrived from Lipa, but he will have to leave again soon. He got stronger there.

In the afternoon at Grandma's, I received a hat and several clay coins. Daddy had overnight duty at the emergency service at the police office, from seven in the evening until a quarter to seven, same as on Friday.

14. XII. 1941 (Sunday)

It is the first day of Chanukah,[20] so I went to see the performance of the parallel class (IV. C). The teacher, Mr. Glanzberg, played the violin; there was singing and theatre. I was invited as class representative of IV. B and I brought a gift for their class representative, Petr Heim, a Young Reader calendar. There were about two hundred gifts that children gave one another (two full laundry baskets). In the evening Daddy went again to the overnight emergency service, in case the police needed something. But so far nothing like that happened, so Daddy sleeps there. He is disturbed by old men playing cards there.

After the school performance Slavek Stein, who hasn't visited us in a long time, walked me home. Afterward I walked him home. On the way we found out that (so they say) people get slapped (Jews, of course), so we tried to hide our stars. Daddy was with the emergency service again, a Jew sang beautifully there, they said he performed in Holland and England as a professional singer.

I heard Jews didn't just get slapped, but terribly beaten up, and some had their entire faces broken by the Vlajkari (Translator's note: name of Czech fascist movement).

20. Chanukah is the eight-day Jewish holiday commemorating the successful revolt of the Maccabees against religious oppression during the reign of Antiochus IV in the second century c.e. The main ritual of the holiday is the lighting of candles.

15. XII. 1941 (Monday)

In the morning at school, many teachers were absent, because they had to write some documents overnight at the Jewish religious community.

A walk in the afternoon. Eva performed in a Chanukah play, she got lots of presents, among them also books and a beautiful jewelry case. In the show she played a grandfather as the prophet Elijah.

16. XII. 1941 (Tuesday)

In the morning at home, around noon at Popper's, where I again bought two books, *The Treasures of Princess Fairy Tale* and *Andersen's Fairy Tales.*

In the afternoon at school, our show, which was supposed to be today, has been moved to Friday.

Today Daddy is not going to the emergency service because instead of ten they are always twelve people there.

We have already lit three Chanukah candles.

17. XII. 1941 (Wednesday)

In the morning at school, the schedule was again all mixed up, because some teachers had to write documents again at the community, all night.

Some German minister arrived in Prague, there was a general street car traffic jam, in some places you couldn't cross the road. This minister's car had the license number ND1.

In the afternoon I had a handicrafts workshop; we are making a bowl for stationery from masking tape. In the early evening I went for a walk near the slaughterhouse. Eva II and Aunt Anda were here.

18. XII. 1941 (Thursday)

In the morning I did my homework, in the afternoon I was at school.

We didn't have any classes at all, just a show. First only for small children, afterward for ourselves. In the children's show there was a magician, a speech, a melodrama, and a game called "In the Toyshop at Midnight." Everything turned out brilliantly; the children received gifts that we (IV. B) had brought them.

Then we performed a show for ourselves; we read all sorts of Chanukah stories and played the accordion. Baum played (nicknamed Little Pasha, because of being fat), and he should be honoured for his talent, and so should Tomas Klein (nicknamed The Eucalyptus Sentence; during an oral exam he once called the Euclid sentence the Eucalyptus sentence), who played a magician and was excellent at it. I personally drew his moustache.

At the end we exchanged presents; I gave Dusner an exploding pencil that blows up when you remove the tip (there is a cap inside).

It was a big success; Miss Lauscherova saw it, too, and laughed very hard.

I got a notebook, pencils, a boat, a geometry set, and lots of other things.

Some time ago they introduced new crown coins (Protectorate ones).

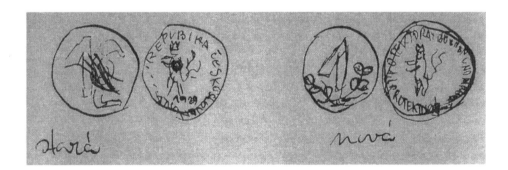

19. XII. 1941 (Friday)

In the morning at school. It's the last day of school, the Christmas break is about to begin. On the way to school my whole heel fell off, so I got to school late because I had to walk slowly. In the afternoon in town; at Orlicky (who sells glass) the workers dropped a big case with glass (about 2 m x 1.5 m x 20 cm) and broke it all. I was watching them carry it outside, but a Jew walked by and told me I'd better go away, because it's a German shop and they could beat me up. It used to be called Ohrenstein & Orlicky (who is a German), but the Germans took the shop away from the Jew Ohrenstein and now it's called just Orlicky.

In the morning Mummy left for Hradec (Kralove) and left us unfortunately a not very precise description of what we should cook.

But we'll manage somehow!

20. XII. 1941 (Saturday)

In the morning I was at Popper's, he's got something wrong with his eyes again and can't go out. (He had scarlet fever, without complications, but since then he's had some sort of eye disease. He used to have a Jewish doctor, but he left for Poland. He has to rub some yellow ointment into his eyes.) That's why I was at his house; we played all kinds of games.

Afterward I walked home, over Maniny under the slaughterhouse.

In the afternoon I visited Grandma.

21. XII. 1941 (Sunday)

In the morning at home, in the afternoon at Grandma's.

We were supposed to meet with the Miloses, but they took a different route (I went to meet [them] to bring them to Grandma's), so we missed each other, and afterward I raced all the way to Perstyn, but it was all in vain. Later we went looking for them in Maniny.

We received a wire from Mummy, saying that she's only coming back on Monday morning.

22. XII. 1941 (Monday)

In the morning at home. In the afternoon we started the preparations for Mancinka's[21] arrival. It's Manci's birthday, but we couldn't get anything, so the presents were quite poor. A quilted hood (so-called tee-pee[22]), a brooch in an inlaid box, stockings, and a sewing kit. Afterward I wanted to cast Mummy's initials in lead, but I didn't succeed.

I made a positive linoleum cut, placed it at the bottom of a bark case, and poured lead into it.

The train was supposed to arrive at 7:15 P.M., but with a delay arrived only at 7:45.

Manci was all upset, her fellow travellers were all thugs and criminals.

Manci brought lots of sweets, pastries, and such. The goose, which M. also brought, weighs 6.60 kg.

I received from Auntie Bozka[23] a flannel shirt as a present; Eva got house slippers.

---

21. We called our mother Mancinka.

22. A separate hood with a pointed tip, tied under the chin.

23. Bozena Sklenckova, Mancinka's sister, Eva II's and Ota's mother.

Hitler is not doing well in Russia, so he removed a general and took his place himself.

23. XII. 1941 (Tuesday)

We just received an announcement from the Jewish Community that we have until December 31 to hand in mouth organs and other portable musical instruments, thermometers and such, cameras and accessories.

In addition we have to register nonportable musical instruments.

In the afternoon at Grandma's.

24. XII. 1941 (Wednesday)

Daddy, Uncle Milos, and Uncle Slava received notification to be prepared to clear away snow when it falls. In the morning at Grandma's, in the afternoon went for a walk with Popper and Eva.

25. XII. 1941 (Thursday)

In the morning at Grandma's; in the afternoon the whole family went to Maniny.

But there was an awful wind, so we had to come back.

In the evening Lianka Kohner came to invite us to come to them at night, as they are lighting their Christmas tree. They have gone completely Aryan.

Mr. Hula was there, the Kohners, the Fiskuses (newlyweds), and Mila Weisbach.

It is snowing; we are all afraid that [the snow] will stay down and Daddy will have to shovel it. Last year he had to do this too, but this time at the Kbelsky airport. The water was very high and Daddy (he was there about 5x) caught a cold there.

Jews will probably have to hand in sweaters again.

26. XII. 1941 (Friday)

In the morning at home, in the afternoon we all went to visit the Levituses, with whom we took a walk on the heath. There we met the Milos family (but without Pavel). They received a new apartment above the Museum; they are incredibly happy. Now they are still subletting (for half a year already) from the Fleischners at 22 Podskalska Street. They have only one room, where there is an office, kitchen, store room, and bedroom, all in one. They sleep mostly on the floor and it is very wretched.—On the way we stopped off at Grandma's.

27. XII. 1941 (Saturday)

In the morning I went for a walk with Popper; it is very windy and cold.
In the afternoon I stayed at home, but Mummy and Daddy went to Grandma's and Eva went for a walk with Renata Hirschova. I had a long enough walk in the morning and aside from that we are expecting a goose from Hradec. Mummy is very worried about the goose going bad on the way here.

28. XII. 1941 (Sunday)

Finally—and we got two geese at once. Mummy sent one to the Levitus family, and gutted the second. It weighed 6.5 kg, it had 420 g of livers, 2¾ kg of lard, and the thighs weighed 870 g. Mummy is all happy about it.
In the afternoon we all went for a walk. In the evening there was a big air attack; the sirens wailed like crazy for half an hour.

29. XII. 1941 (Monday)

Miss Lauscherova invited us (or rather ordered us) to Hagibor, so I went, but it was no fun for me; there was skating and I didn't have any skates, so I just froze there. The whole area was filled with huge heaps of church benches, which had been brought from all the synagogues, and Jews working as forced laborers were breaking them up into firewood.

As I walked home from Hagibor, I saw lots of announcements put up everywhere, that you have to hand in skis longer than 180 cm (even Aryans), but Jews have to give it away for free and Aryans will get a compensation. But they also have to report for snow-clearing duty (for now they just have to be prepared).—At home in the afternoon.

30. XII. 1941 (Tuesday)

In the morning at Grandma's and in town.

Grandma received a goose and is therefore very happy.

In the afternoon I went for a walk.

31. XII. 1941 (Wednesday)

It is the last day of this year.

In the morning I did my homework; in the afternoon I went for a walk with Popper. The Vltava is partly frozen. At five o'clock Grandma's family came to visit and stayed until late at night. Afterward, when they left, Mummy and Daddy went next door to the Kohners and celebrated New Year's Eve until one thirty at night, then they came back and went to sleep. But in the morning they slept in until 10 o'clock. (Actually, this belongs to the next day.)

1. I. 1942 (Thursday)

I made myself a nice violin from bark, but I don't yet know how to play it, because so far it has only two (rubber) strings.

In the morning I did my homework. Otherwise nothing special. Actually, a lot is happening, but it is not even visible. What is quite ordinary now would certainly cause upset in a normal time. For example, Jews don't have fruit, geese, and any poultry, cheese, onions, garlic, and many other things. Tobacco ration cards are forbidden to prisoners, madmen, and Jews. They are not allowed to travel in the front section of trams, buses, trolleybuses; they are not allowed to take walks on riverbanks, etc., etc.

2. I. 1942 (Friday)

In the morning I did my homework, in the afternoon went for a walk.

3. I. 1942 (Saturday)

In the morning at Popper's; he has a runny nose again and is in bed.

In the afternoon at Grandma's. I heard that the Germans suddenly entered Jepa (a department store), closed it, and whoever was wearing warm galoshes had their identity cards taken away and the galoshes stamped, so that they will have to go and hand them in. Then they'll get their identity cards back.

They say that in Brno they were taking them away right there in the streets. So now everyone is afraid of it.

Petr GINZ

Today it's clear to everyone
who is a Jew and who's an Aryan,
because you'll know Jews near and far
by their black and yellow star.
And Jews who are so demarcated
must live according to the rules dictated:

Always, after eight o'clock,
be at home and click the lock;
work only labouring with pick or hoe,
and do not listen to the radio.
You're not allowed to own a mutt;
barbers can't give your hair a cut;
a female Jew who once was rich
can't have a dog, even a bitch,
she cannot send her kids to school
must shop from three to five since that's the rule.

She can't have bracelets, garlic, wine,
or go to the theatre, out to dine;
she can't have cars or a gramophone,
fur coats or skis or a telephone;
she can't eat onions, pork, or cheese,
have instruments, or matrices;
she cannot own a clarinet

or keep a canary for a pet,
rent bicycles or barometers,
have woollen socks or warm sweaters.

And especially the outcast Jew
must give up all habits he knew:
he can't buy clothes, can't buy a shoe,
since dressing well is not his due;
he can't have poultry, shaving soap,
or jam or anything to smoke;
can't get a license, buy some gin,
read magazines, a news bulletin,
buy sweets or a machine to sew;
to fields or shops he cannot go
even to buy a single pair
of winter woollen underwear,
or a sardine or a ripe pear.

And if this list is not complete
there's more, so you should be discreet;
don't buy a thing; accept defeat.

Walk everywhere you want to go
in rain or sleet or hail or snow.
Don't leave your house, don't push a pram,
don't take a bus or train or tram;
you're not allowed on a fast train;
don't hail a taxi, or complain;

no matter how thirsty you are
you must not enter any bar;
the riverbank is not for you,
or a museum or park or zoo
or swimming pool or stadium or
post office or department store,
or church, casino, or cathedral
or any public urinal.
And you be careful not to use
main streets, and keep off avenues!
And if you want to breathe some air
go to God's garden and walk there
among the graves in the cemetery
because no park to you is free.

And if you are a clever Jew
you'll close off bank accounts and you
will give up other habits too
like meeting Aryans you knew.

He used to be allowed a swag,
suitcase, rucksack, or carpetbag.
Now he has lost even those rights
but every Jew lowers his sights
and follows all the rules he's got
and doesn't care one little jot.

4. I. 1942 (Sunday)

In the morning homework, in the afternoon a walk.

5. I. 1942 (Monday)

In the morning in town, in the afternoon at Grandma's.

6. I. 1942 (Tuesday)

In the morning with Popper, in the afternoon at Grandma's.
Uncle Milos has an inflammation of the periosteum.

7. I. 1942 (Wednesday)

In the morning in town, in the afternoon went for a walk.

8. I. 1942 (Thursday)

In the morning at home, in the afternoon a walk; the Miloses came to visit us,
but without Aunt Nada.

9. I. 1942 (Friday)

In the morning in town. Mr. Weisbach came here for a visit and told us how
he was locked in jail for ten days, because his identity card didn't say "J."
He said the director (former of course) from Kolben-Danek was there, and
also many other Jews.

10. I. 1942 (Saturday)

In the morning went for a walk with Popper, in the afternoon at Grandma's.

11. I. 1942 (Sunday)

Homework in the morning, in the afternoon I went with Eva, Renata Hirschova (Eva's friend), sleigh-riding in Maniny.

We received an order to hand in fur coats, everything made of fur, wool undergarments, pullovers, etc. Only one set of underwear is allowed per person. There is a big collection to help soldiers on the front, they are collecting warm underwear, a special announcement is published about it every day. I heard that so far three thousand train carriages have been sent to the front.

12. I. 1942 (Monday)

Today we had to hand in one sweater; some Jews carried to the collection centres huge parcels with fur coats, underwear, and other things. There they are loaded into moving trucks and and it's still not enough and there are mountains of parcels everywhere.

In the afternoon in town.

13. I. 1942 (Tuesday)

In the morning I went for a walk with Popper. It's terribly cold.

14. I. 1942 (Wednesday)

In the morning at home; in the afternoon I went with Daddy and Eva sleighriding in Maniny. They say that the Maniny sewer will soon be completely filled; now they are dumping rubbish from all of Prague into it. It's already half full.

Some boys found metal sawdust among the rubbish and also a bottle of carbide and in the evening (during blackout) they started such a big fire that you could see it all over Prague. When the bottles with carbide blew up it shook all of Maniny. Then a policeman discovered them and when he reached them, a huge flash burst out of the fire, which annoyed the policeman to the highest degree.

15. I. 1942 (Thursday)
In the morning at home. In the afternoon with Popper; they just took away Mrs. Popperova's registered sewing machine, which makes her very unhappy.

16. I. 1942 (Friday)
In the morning at home, in the afternoon went for a walk in town.

17. I. 1942 (Saturday)
In the morning at home, in the afternoon at Grandma's.

18. I. 1942 (Sunday)
In the morning at home, in the afternoon at Grandma's with the Miloses. All mixed marriages received questionnaires to fill out.

19. I. 1942 (Monday)
In the morning in town, in the afternoon at home.

20. I. 1942 (Tuesday)
I heard they've formed a new government, and Moravec, who writes agitating articles, is the minister for education.
In the morning at Popper's; Turna was there, too.
In the afternoon went walking in Troja, it's awfully cold (at least −19°C for sure); Eva cried all the way home because she was freezing.

21. I. 1942 (Wednesday)

In the morning at home and in town, in the afternoon at home.
Slavek Stein came to visit.

22. I. 1942 (Thursday)

In the morning at home, in the afternoon in town and on a walk.
There are new transports to Theresienstadt; Mrs. Traub is going too. That's why I was at the Poppers, to check if they were going as well, because many people whose names start with P were called up.
There are notices up everywhere in the streets saying the new Czech government believes in the victory of the Reich, etc., etc.

23. I. 1942 (Friday)

From two o'clock in the afternoon until six there is no electricity or gas, trams usually have only one car. Our lift is not working.
In the afternoon at the Levituses. Uncle is writing lots of documents for Mrs. Traubova for the move to Theresienstadt. I heard that in Theresienstadt they have also interned Frenchmen, Poles, and other foreigners (non-Jews). Supposedly eight people were executed there for trying to escape.

24. I. 1942 (Saturday)

In the morning I went for a walk with Popper; in the afternoon I stayed home.

25. I. 1942 (Sunday)

In the morning at home; in the afternoon we all went for a walk in Maniny.

26. I. 1942 (Monday)

In the morning in town. Today from three in the afternoon Jews are not allowed to travel by tram. The only exceptions are people older than sixty, Jewish Community employees, and so on.

The Miloses are moving into their new apartment in Vinohrady.

27. I. 1942 (Tuesday)

The Milos family slept in their new apartment for the first time.

In the morning in town, in the afternoon at home; trams get stuck in snowdrifts.

28. I. 1942 (Wednesday)

In the morning in town, Mr. Tausig was here. In the afternoon at home.

The Goldmanns from Budyne are leaving for Theresienstadt.

29. I. 1942 (Thursday)

In the morning at home, in the afternoon as well. Uncle Slava has been forced to shovel snow for many days already; he doesn't even have proper shoes and he's freezing.

30. I. 1942 (Friday)

Daddy caught a cold this morning while carrying coal, because he went in his shirt across the hall to the storage room. He saw Dr. Slezak, who sent him to the Jewish Dr. Lang.

31. I. 1942 (Saturday)

Daddy is feeling very ill, he can't breathe out, on the way to the doctor he almost fainted, so for the way back he had to give Daddy an injection.

He's got pleuritis.

In the afternoon at Grandma's, it's her name-day. Daddy couldn't go there (12 Vojtesska Street), because he has to lie down in a warm bed. Grandma gave us excellent cakes baked by Aunt Anda.

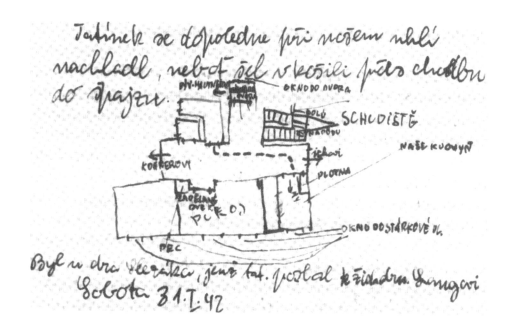

1. II. 1942 (Sunday)

Today is my birthday, I got lots of things:

1. a Christmas cake from Mummy
2. an empty book for writing in from Ota
3. wrist warmers from Eva
4. figs from Mummy
5. marbles (sweets, made by Mummy)
6. oranges
7. sweets
8. borrowed books: Verne—*Big Chaos,* Nekola— *The Thirteenth Governor,* Stevenson—*Treasure Island*
9. a small notebook from Eva
10. five Ex-fizzy sweets from Manci
11. a packet of sweets from Eva Sklenckova
12. gingerbreads from Mummy (ox eyes)
13. a handkerchief
14. orange peel
15. 100 crowns from Grandma
16. fine tea biscuits from Grandma
17. a packet of biscuits from the Miloses

Daddy is feeling a bit better.—The Miloses were here in the afternoon.

2. II. 1942 (Monday)

In the morning at home, and in the afternoon, too.

3. II. 1942 (Tuesday)

In the morning in town, in the afternoon at home.

At half past eleven at night a messenger from the Community came to tell us that Daddy has to report to the exhibition ground on Thursday morning. He was registered as a car mechanic, and that's why they chose Daddy, in spite of the mixed marriage. There was a terrible rush, we were preparing everything for the journey, the Kohners were helping us. Fortunately, Daddy got a fever and Dr. Lang, who was called in by the Community, sent a message to the Community that Daddy is unable to join the transport. Of course we were very pleased.

4. II. 1942 (Wednesday)

Daddy is fine, he just wheezes from time to time.

5. II. 1942 (Thursday)

A huge number of our friends have been called up for the new transport: Bardach, Mr. Mautner (an acquaintance of Uncle Karel), Hirschova, who used to go for walks with Eva, and many others.

6. II. 1942 (Friday)

In the morning in town, in the afternoon at home.

7. II. 1942 (Saturday)

In the morning at home, in the afternoon with Popper.

8. II. 1942 (Sunday)

Bardach came to say goodbye to me, he and his whole family are going on Monday to the exhibition grounds (leaving for Theresienstadt).

In the afternoon the Miloses were here, they brought me a packet of sweets, it's still for my birthday.

9. II. 1942 (Monday)

In the morning in town; W. Adler was here and brought an invitation to come to school, because we've had no classes since December 19 and the holidays have been extended.

10. II. 1942 (Tuesday)

In the morning I was in school, where I found out that I have been assigned to study group B.

11. II. 1942 (Wednesday)

Daddy is feeling a little worse. In the morning my group met at the Goldsteins; we were given a huge amount of homework; in the afternoon I went for a walk.

12. II. 1942 (Thursday)

In the morning in town, in the afternoon at Grandma's.

13. II. 1942 (Friday)

In the morning I was with Popper, in the afternoon at Grandma's.

14. II. 1942 (Saturday)

In the morning at home, in the afternoon at Grandma's.

15. II. 1942 (Sunday)

In the morning at home; I made a new linocut.

16. II. 1942 (Monday)

In the morning in town, in the afternoon at the Miloses to see their apartment for the first time. It is cold there. Pavel and Uncle were in the middle of re-doing the kitchen; it was an awful mess. They divided the kitchen into two parts and turned one into a bathroom.

17. II. 1942 (Tuesday)

In the morning at home, in the afternoon went for a walk.

18. II. 1942 (Wednesday)

In the morning with Popper. Daddy is feeling somewhat better.

19. II. 1942 (Thursday)

In the morning at home, in the afternoon on a walk.

For a long time now, groups of Jews can be seen clearing the snow off the streets; Uncle Slava goes to shovel it every single day and the skin on his hands is cracked from frost.

20. II. 1942 (Friday)

In the morning I met with my study group at the Adlers at 13 Krakovska Street. We had Dr. Reich, who was once slapped by a German.

I heard that some local people wanted to kill a turkey, but they felt sorry for it and didn't want to just cut its throat, so they gave it Veronal, plucked it, and put it in water. But then the dear turkey woke up and because it was cold without feathers, they knitted a sweater for it, and so it now walks around in a sweater. In the afternoon I went for a walk. In the afternoon Eva II came to visit us.

21. II. 1942 (Saturday)

It's Eva's birthday. She got lots of stuff:

1. a cake
2. pastry cigars
3. sweets (toffees, jelly sweets, raspberries—3 bags)
4. a box with Odkolek sweets
5. sweets with a red rose
6. a piece of Turkish delight
7. a packet of fizzy sweets
8. a box of biscuits from Eva II
9. a hood
10. an empty book for writing
11. ex libris
12. a photo album
13. a comb
14. a chain
15. three borrowed books: *Black India, Spicka Wants to Be a Reporter, Mila Vetroplach*
16. 100 crowns

22. II. 1942 (Sunday)

In the morning I was at the Miloses, in the afternoon I stayed home and also went for a walk.

23. II. 1942 (Monday)

In the morning in town, in the afternoon at home. Dr. Slezak was here. He recommended that we put Daddy in the hospital, because he is worse.

Family Photos

The antique shop in Prague's Jungmann Square that belonged to Petr and Eva's grandfather, Josef Ginz.

Marie Dolanska (Mancinka) and Otto Ginz in their wedding photo, March 8, 1927.

The Ginz family near their summer apartment in Strasin, August 1931.

The Ginz family in February 1933—Eva and Petr in
foreground, Mancinka and Otto behind them.

Eva and Petr Ginz, 1934.

Petr and Eva Ginz on the embankment, Prague, spring 1936.

The Ginz family on Prikopy Street, spring 1938.

The Ginz family in 1939.

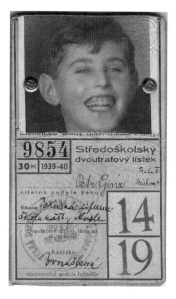

Winter in Podoli (from left: Petr, Eva, Mancinka, Mrs. Traubova and Herma Levitusova).

Petr's identification for the streetcar from 1939, when he attended the first year of a general school in Nusle; because of his Jewish origins, he had to leave this school.

Sitting, from left: Milos Ginz, his wife Nada, Mancinka, Eva Sklenckova; behind them: Petr Ginz and Pavel Ginz (Milos and Nada's son).

Petr Ginz's Diary

from the twenty-fourth of February
of the year nineteen hundred and forty-two
(Tuesday)
until————[24]

---

24. The diary ends with the entry of August 8, 1942, a month before Petr's transport to Theresienstadt.

24. II. 1942 (Tuesday)

In the morning I was at home; in the afternoon a car came from the Health Insurance to take Daddy to the Jewish hospital on Lublanska Street. The car was beautiful, modern, and very springy. It arrived at about 3.30 P.M.
The Miloses could have been poisoned by a gas leak.

25. II. 1942 (Wednesday)

German flags at the Hybernske train station and in front of the winter stadium. In the morning with my study group at the Goldmanns, 46 Na Porici; we were given lots and lots of homework.—In the afternoon at home and on a walk. The snow is melting, so there is a thaw, during which Jews sweep the wet snow. At Maniny. In the evening we received a parcel from Aunt Bozka. There was cream cheese in it and an orange for Mummy; and linocuts for me. The prints of the cuts arrived in the afternoon by post.

26. II. 1942 (Thursday)

In the morning I was in town. There was a bomb assassination against some Papen, a friend of the Germans.
In the afternoon we went to visit Daddy in the hospital. It is in the same place where Mrs. Kohner lived when she was little (an orphanage).
It is very nice there. Daddy is by the window on the first floor on the right; you have to walk through one room and there it is. There are five beds. When we arrived, a young man was shaving Daddy.—Then Uncle Milos came, too, and then we left and went to visit them.

27. II. 1942 (Friday)

Because I noticed yesterday that my gums were swollen and I had a bump behind the ear, I went to the Jewish ambulatory clinic on Vezenska Street, with my identity card. They rubbed some liquid into the gums and told me to come back on Monday. As for the bump, I am supposed to come to the surgery at 4:30 in the afternoon.

The Kohners received a letter from Theresienstadt from Leo (the fat one). He writes that they are healthy; they are allowed to write only thirty words, in block capitals, and send it through the Jewish Community.

28. II. 1942 (Saturday)

In the morning in town; in the afternoon I brougt Daddy a package and left it with the porter. Daddy is in No. 18; Dr. Pollak is in the room next door. He's the annoying fat man who wrote "Rivka Is Getting Married." He is currently the minister for Jewish education.

In the streets there are masses of Germans and frequent parades with drumming. Today they punctured Daddy's exudate. Daddy is feeling better.

1. III. 1942 (Sunday)

In the morning I stayed at home and helped Mummy. In the afternoon I visited Daddy in the hospital. Large groups of Hitlerjugend are now forming in front of our house, so there is a lot of shouting.

They removed three litres of water from Daddy's lungs! They dragged some containers to him, lots of doctors came running, even the chief doctor Klein himself, and the puncture was done quite painlessly. They asked him: Shall we make it a full three liters?

Daddy told them: Do help yourselves.

There is also a man there who is dying of cancer.

2. III. 1942 (Monday)

In the morning in town, in the afternoon at home. Mummy is gone with Eva and Eva II to the Zink auction in the Beranek hotel, and because the laundry is supposed to get picked up any minute by the Seiners, I have to stay at home. Slavek came in the afternoon to tell me I have to be in school the day after tomorrow for my exams.

3. III. 1942 (Tuesday)

In the afternoon in town. There are ordinances everywhere saying that it is not allowed to wash Jewish laundry. The exhibition "Soviet paradise" began on Saturday, [February] 28. In many shop windows they are exhibiting seized Russian helmets, cannons, and gas masks.

4. III. 1942 (Wednesday)

In the afternoon at school. We had a test in music; I didn't know anything, but I was clever enough to copy it. Afterward I had an oral exam in natural history and [we took] a math test.
In the afternoon I was outdoors with Slavek.

5. III. 1942 (Thursday)

In the afternoon I was in town and at the dental ambulatory clinic on Kelly's [street] (U stare skoly),[25] because of the abscess that has been forming on my gums for a long time now.
In the afternoon at home.

25. Translator's note: U stare skoly = By the Old School; this is the original Czech name of the street, changed to Kelly's Street under the Nazi regime.

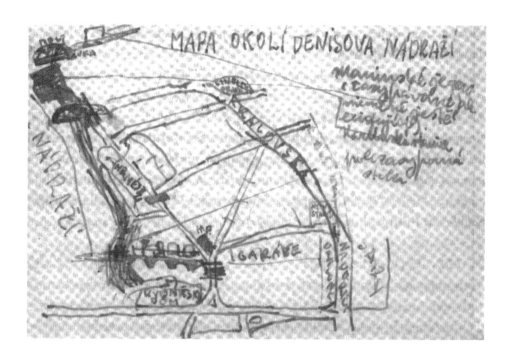

6. III. 1942 (Friday)

There was a terrible air raid on Paris; I heard there were 220–250 dead and over a thousand injured (see 11.III.)

In the morning in town, in the afternoon on a walk with Popper.

7. III. 1942 (Saturday)

In the morning in town and in the afternoon at home.

In the evening I went for a walk. The water in the river is far below the normal level, so from the embankment you can see the stairs to the lower river bank, from the lower bank to the edge of the bulwark, and five steps of the ladder below.

8. III. 1942 (Sunday)

In the morning I was at home; in the afternoon I went for a walk and to visit Daddy in the hospital.

The doctor who looked after him now has pneumonia himself.

The Japanese have seriously threatened Java.

9. III. 1942 (Monday)

In the morning at school, they told us our approximate results on the report card. I will probably get a B in music, a B (c) [in] maths and a B [in] geography.—In the afternoon at home.

10. III. 1942 (Tuesday)

In the morning in town, in the afternoon at school.

We are not allowed to travel by tram No. 1, because the most frequent disturbances between Jews and Germans go on there. It is possible that Jews will not be allowed to travel at all (even with identity cards).

11. III. 1942 (Wednesday)

In the morning at school; they counted 750 casualties in Paris and 1,400 injured.—In the afternoon outside.

12. III. 1942 (Thursday)

In the morning I was in town; there is an announcement on the board in Politika in Wenceslav Square that Jews are not allowed to read newspapers. In the afternoon at school.

13. III. 1942 (Friday)

In the morning at school; we received our report cards, in two languages of course, even our marks were written in Czech and in German. Except for a B in handwriting, maths, geography, and music, I have all A's.

In the afternoon with Daddy. I slipped in without the porter noticing and made it all the way to Daddy's room, handed in the parcel, and had to quickly run away so the nurses wouldn't find me there.

Because it wasn't visiting time.

14. III. 1942 (Saturday)

In the morning in town.

In the afternoon on a walk with Popper. He and I are trying to make an element that will produce electricity, using a solution with blue vitriol (of copper) and a solution of bitter salt (with zinc).

We failed, because the two solutions blended with each other.

15. III. 1942 (Sunday)

We received a note, saying that tomorrow at 9 o'clock the Sklenckas will arrive from Hradec.

I visited Daddy in the hospital in the afternoon. He is feeling a bit better.

16. III. 1942 (Monday)

The Sklenckas arrived. Eva II was here in the afternoon. They slept over at our house (not Eva II, of course). Uncle spent a long time at the bank in the morning.

In the afternoon I was outside.

17. III. 1942 (Tuesday)

Josef Svatopluk Machar died.

In the morning I was at home and in town, in the afternoon at school.

We were shooting paper balls even during lessons. I bought one coupon for the "Trigo" competition for 20 heller; you have to guess how to play the game Trigo and attach the coupon to the answer. Then you get all the coins that were chosen.

18. III. 1942 (Wednesday)

In the morning at school.

Daddy phoned to say that he is supposed to come home from the hospital at 3 o'clock this afternoon. Of course it has caused a big commotion. We could have burned the house down, because a hot piece of coal fell out of the stove, Aunt Bozka and Eva didn't notice it, and some papers caught fire.—Aunt Herma broke her arm.

19. III. 1942 (Thursday)

In the morning in town, in the afternoon at school.

20. III. 1942 (Friday)

They arrested all the Americans who are Jews.

In the morning at school, in the afternoon outside. As far as I know, there was loose ice floating on the river; I haven't been able to get to the embankment, so I don't know for sure.

21. III. 1942 (Saturday)

In the morning in town, in the afternoon at Popper's. This time the two solutions didn't blend like last time, but the element still didn't work.

In Maniny there was a huge collection of bells taken from churches.

You could see forty-one bells, but around the bend there were more, small and enormous ones, so that there could have been eighty to a hundred of them. I once saw in Strossmayer place how they took it down from the tower.

22. III. 1942 (Sunday)

Uncle Milos also has to sweep snow, even though the bone membrane (periosteum) in his hand is inflamed. Uncle Slava has been doing it for eight weeks already and he has huge blisters and terribly cracked hands.

In the morning at home; in the afternoon I started translating the story "Die Nacht auf dem Walfisch"[26] by Gerstäckr.

23. III. 1942 (Monday)

Daddy was X-rayed at the Bernard.

In the morning at school; in the afternoon at home.

24. III. 1942 (Tuesday)

In the morning in town, in the afternoon at school.

I also had an oral in natural history. I probably got an A, an A minus in the worst case.

25. III. 1942 (Wednesday)

In the morning at school, in the afternoon at home and in town.

Daddy's X-ray results (see 23.III.) were very satisfactory.

Soon he will be able to go out for a short walk.

He lost about 12 kg.—I have a permit to travel by tram for three weeks.

26. "The Night on the Whale."

26. III. 1942 (Thursday)

In the morning in town, in the afternoon at school. I was tested in religion[27] by Elisa Stein (1–2).

27. III. 1942 (Friday)

In the morning in school. In the afternoon outdoors.
Auntie Nepomericka is going to Theresienstadt.

28. III. 1942 (Saturday)

In the morning with Popper. Eva was at Grandma's in the afternoon.
I heard that already at 1:30 the gas supply was very weak (at two it is supposed to be stopped altogether) and at the Miloses there was no gas at all. We want to light our gas—and here it's also gone! So we don't know how to cook our dinner.
In the afternoon with Popper, in Maniny there are still huge numbers of church bells: it is forbidden to take photos of them. They are gradually being removed. We received a flyer.[28]

29. III. 1942 (Sunday)

In the morning at home.—You can't hear any bells ringing at all, because the Germans have confiscated them all; they will probably make cannons out of them. They left only the Zikmund on St. Vitus and that's the only church bell in Prague now.

---

27. One of the subjects at school was religious education.

28. A flyer was inserted in the diary "An Dich, Prager Hausfrau—For You, Prague House-wives!" calling for the collection of kitchen waste and rubbish.

In the afternoon in Troja. The Vltava is overflowing, but I still saw a ferry crossing it, loaded with about thirty people.

It's still pretty cold, but the sun is already shining nicely.

30. III. 1942 (Monday)

In the morning at school, in the afternoon outside.

They were taking the bell out of Tyn Cathedral.

31. III. 1942 (Tuesday)

In the morning in town; in the afternoon at school, we had a maths test and German composition.

1. IV. 1942 (Wednesday)

In the morning at school. Because it was April Fool's Day, we wanted to trick the teacher Mr. Beinkoles with an exploding pencil, but our attempt failed and B. confiscated our pencil with capsules. That's how our 1st of April turned out. In the afternoon outside.

2. IV. 1942 (Thursday)

In the morning in town.

It is the first day of the Easter and at the same time the Pesach holidays.[29]

I borrowed a book by Jules Verne, *The Secret of the Deep Forest*.

Ota Fiser (the confectioner) has been moved out of Benesov, or not exactly from Benesov, because he was felling forest trees with some other Jews.

He was sent to Dobris. They are also moving people out of Neveklov (Aryans, too); Germans will be arriving there.

---

29. Pesach, or Passover, is the Jewish holiday commemorating the Jews' exodus from slavery in Egypt in about 1235 B.C.E. The holiday begins with a festive meal called a seder.

3. IV. 1942 (Friday)

In the morning at home and in town, in the afternoon outside.

4. IV. 1942 (Saturday)

In the morning on a walk with Popper, in the afternoon at home.

5. IV. 1942 (Sunday)

With Auntie Anda in Maniny, across the ferry under the cliff under Bulovka. Auntie wanted to visit Vilma Tapferova, but she has already gone to Theresienstadt.

The apartment was locked and covered with the stickers of "Treuhandstelle."[30]

6. IV. 1942 (Monday)

In the morning at home, in the afternoon on an outing to Dablice.

7. IV. 1942 (Tuesday)

Ota Fiser arrived from Dobris, because he has been forced to move out, together with people from Neveklov.

He has to go to Tabor to register. He spent the night at our place.

8. IV. 1942 (Wednesday)

I lost the diary and don't remember what happened.
Ota Fiser has left.

30. Translator's note: The so-called *Treuhandstelle* was founded by the Nazi authorities. It was an organization attached to the Prague Jewish Community whose task was to collect and store the property of deportees.

9. IV. 1942 (Thursday)

Ota Fiser came back from Tabor.

He said he'll be leaving for Theresienstadt in the beginning of May.

10. IV. 1942 (Friday)

In the morning at school, in the afternoon outside.

11. IV. 1942 (Saturday)

In the morning in town.

In the afternoon with Popper in Maniny. There are at least two thousand bells there. They keep filling up the Maniny sewer.

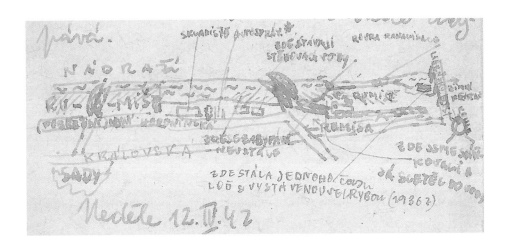

12. IV. 1942 (Sunday)

I visited the Levituses, who gave me lots of small things.

They have no fat whatsoever and Auntie Herma is complaining terribly.

13. IV. 1942 (Monday)

In the morning at school. They announced the new transport and it's all names with Löv-, Löw-, Lev-, and so on. So we were worried about the Levituses, because I heard they are now taking mainly people with more property. I dropped by there in the afternoon, aunt was at the doctor's to have her bandage taken off, they are not leaving.

14. IV. 1942 (Tuesday)

It is allowed to fill sausages with dog meat. The Blochs (people we know) had for a special roast the meat of a crow! Daddy visited Grandma for the first time since he became ill.

Since yesterday the gas supply is back to normal.

The Vaneks arrived—without uncle and Lidunka, because they have to work in the office. Verka came too—with little Eva Sidlova; she speaks quite well already and walks like a grown-up. She wears a little ponytail and loves to chat. She is always telling you something, first, that she is called Alkova (Alka is her doll's name) and then that she is the aunt from Horice, and kisses you accordingly.

15. IV. 1942 (Wednesday)

In the morning at school, we had a Machar-party, to which we invited other classes. It was a success.—Mancinka's face is terribly swollen, you can't recognize her. She met several acquaintances on the street and no one recognized her. I heard it's from all those food substitutes.

16. IV. 1942 (Thursday)

Mummy's swelling hasn't gone down yet.

In the morning from 9:30 to 11 at Hagibor. We exercised in shirts, that's why we had to have the stars sewn onto them, too. So I had three stars on top of one another: on my overcoat, my coat, and my shirt.

In the afternoon at school: a performance of [Erben's] "Kytice" ("Bouquet"). Also wasn't bad; better than that Machar.—The Vaneks left at 4:45.

17. IV. 1942 (Friday)

In the afternoon at school, our teacher Mr. Sommer is leaving with the transport for Theresienstadt and from our class Bärova and Rita Goldmannova. Then on Monday at 6 o'clock in the morning Uncle Slava and Uncle Milos are leaving to work on the motorway in Krivoklat. In the afternoon at home. Last night someone from the Community came hammering on our door again: transport! Of course, Daddy will appeal it right away.

18. IV. 1942 (Saturday)

The men who go to Krivoklat get paid 1,000 crowns a month and they are also allowed weekly home visits. Those from the last group have come back already and will go again.

In the morning in town, in the afternoon at home.

Daddy was at the Community for a check-up.

19. IV. 1942 (Sunday)

Tokyo, Yokohama, Kobe, and many other Japanese cities were heavily bombed by the Americans.

In the morning at home; in the afternoon we had a visit from the Miloses and from Grandma.

20. IV. 1942 (Monday)

At 6 o'oclock in the morning Uncles Slava and Milos left for Moriny near Karlstejn (not Krivoklat).—In the morning at home and in town (there was a throng of people in front of the Main—Wilson's train station), in the afternoon as well. Hitler is fifty-three years old; there are flags and parades everywhere and his bust is in every shop window. Every building has to hang out a swastika flag, except for Jews, of course, who are not allowed this pleasure. It is strictly forbidden to them.

In the afternoon with Daddy in Smichov. Afterward we went to say good-bye to Mr. Felix Lederer from Petrske Square. He is leaving tomorrow morning already for Theresienstadt. The Friedländers are supposed to go, too, even though Mr. Friedländer just had a stroke.

21. IV. 1942 (Tuesday)

Yesterday's commotion in front of Wilson's train station was a way of handing over the ambulance train by Hacha to Heydrich, as Adolf Hitler's representative. Frank and many others were there, too.

In the morning in town, in the afternoon at school (the result of my maths composition: B/B). I was wearing only a coat and a massive downpour broke out. I got soaked to the bone and my shirt was all wet.

The drain in front of our house was blocked, which created a big lake.

And as I was running, I stepped right into it—tap, tap! Lucky it was in front of our house.

22. IV. 1942 (Wednesday)

In the morning at school, in the afternoon at home and with Popper. From our class Zinn and Stern are leaving. Baum (The Fat One) was supposed to go, but came back from the exhibition ground.

23. IV. 1942 (Thursday)

In the morning in town. Leaves are budding everywhere and grass has been green for a long time. In the afternoon at school.
In the evening I broke a lamp by throwing a pillow.

24. IV. 1942 (Friday)

In the morning at school. In the afternoon at home and outdoors with Daddy.

25. IV. 1942 (Saturday)

In the morning at Grandma's. Uncles Slava and Milos came from work; it is miserable there: there is no water, so they have to bring it from far away. In the building, where there are about three hundred of them; there is a leak at the top and at the bottom and Uncle Milos caught a cold from it. And Slava, for a change, has a bandaged finger. They were smashing gravel and as they were loading it (the rocks) onto a cart, a clumsy man let go of it (the rock) too soon and Uncle's hand got caught underneath it.
Before they got there, Aryan workers were doing forty carts a day and now that the Jews are there they are doing forty as well. And then they say that with Jews and without [it's] the same, while they're lazy as hell themselves. They make the Jews remove the earth between the rocks and then, after half their job has been done by the Jews, they show off how many carts of gravel they

brought and how many were brought by the Jews. Their leader is always threatening them (the Jews) that at first they will be corrected (?!), then reprimanded, and finally, if they refuse to work, they will be excluded.

Dr. Bloch, who treated Daddy, is leaving for Theresienstadt.

There have just been two transports one after another.

26. IV. 1942 (Sunday)

In the morning at home, in the afternoon on a walk.

Early this morning before 1:30 the English were near Prague; there was an alarm. As I found out later (27. IV.), they were over Pilsen and dropped a few bombs there.

27. IV. 1942 (Monday)

In the morning at school, in the afternoon outside.

Zinn from our class, who was supposed to leave with a transport, came back, because he was ill at the time.—Another alarm last night.

28. IV. 1942 (Tuesday)

In the morning in town.

In the afternoon at school. Ivan Dusner from our class is leaving for Theresienstadt.

29. IV. 1942 (Wednesday)

In the morning at school; we will be making a barometer, which will always show the weather one day ahead.

In Boys' Handicrafts, I also handed in the exercise book covers that we started last lesson and finished at home. I got an A. Again there was an alarm last night.

30. IV. 1942 (Thursday)

In the morning in town, in the afternoon at school; during measuring class and especially maths (Mr. Lauder) there was a terrible bombardment. Fives were raining down on us.

1. V. 1942 (Friday)

In the morning at school, Miss Lauscherova is ill, so we've been having fewer classes for several days in a row.

In the afternoon at home; Hansi was here and we played marbles. I lost.

2. V. 1942 (Saturday)

In the morning I went for a walk with Popper; there are over eight thousand numbered church bells in Maniny and many unnumbered ones.

In the afternoon at home. The Hirsches (the shoemaker) are leaving (actually, they left a long time ago but I only just found out), with Margitka, the one who said that she will vomit here.

3. V. 1942 (Sunday)

In the morning at home, I was doing graphs and other homework.

In the afternoon I was with Eva and Daddy in Maniny. It is now almost the only place where Jews can go for a walk, so it is full of them, even though about twenty thousand have already left Prague.

4. V. 1942 (Monday)

In the morning at school, in the afternoon at home.—There was an alarm again at night.

5. V. 1942 (Tuesday)

In the morning at home and outside; in the afternoon at school. I organized a lottery to help Zinn, who has tuberculosis. A ticket costs 50 hellers and you can win 5, 3, and 2 crowns.

6. V. 1942 (Wednesday)

In the morning at school. I was selling the lottery tickets; I sold all one hundred of them! In the afternoon I printed another 150 (then I realized that I had made a mistake in the numbering. I wrote: 120, 121, 122, 133, 135, 136, etc.—so I handed out only 140 + 100 tickets).
I met up with Popper.

7. V. 1942 (Thursday)

In the morning I went to Hagibor for school physical education. It was terribly boring there for those who don't play football. In the afternoon at school; I was selling lottery tickets again and hired Singer and Jelinek from IV.A for this purpose (that's where Pavel is, too; he was also helping me sell tickets).

8. V. 1942 (Friday)

In the morning at school. I finished selling all the tickets and handed in over 110 crowns for Zinn. The draw took place with the participation of Mr. Reich and Miss Lauscherova. The whole class was packed with people from IV.A, B, and C. Then I brought a tiny child who was terribly scared among the giants from IV.A (who wanted to lynch me already and were screaming like mad, "When is the draw?"); I tied a (dirty) handkerchief around his eyes and mixed the numbered pieces of paper in a hat.

The child drew:

3rd prize, 2 crowns (number 54)—absent,

2nd prize, 3 crowns (number 1, unusual!)—Punta from our class, gave it up for the benefit of Zinn's fund,

and

(great excitement)

1st prize, 10 crowns (number 16)—Birnbaum from IV.A, who gave up half of it for the benefit of Zinn's fund.

I did the draw after lessons.—In the afternoon outside.

9. V. 1942 (Saturday)

In the morning on a walk with Popper, in the afternoon at Grandma's. Again, Uncles Milos and Slava came for a visit, as usual. Uncle Slava shaved all his hair. They are both complaining about too much work.

10. V. 1942 (Sunday)

In the morning at home, in the afternoon on a walk.

11. V. 1942 (Monday)

From today on there are rations for vegetables.

In the morning at school, in the afternoon outside.

12. V. 1942 (Tuesday)

In the morning in town, in the afternoon at school.

I was tested in German.

13. V. 1942 (Wednesday)

In the morning at school.

300 crowns were stolen from Fischhoffova in girls' PE.

I am attaching an example of how newspapers write today (Narodni politika).[31]

14. V. 1942 (Thursday)

In the morning at home and outside.

I was studying really hard, because and for the reason that I will volunteer to be tested in geography on Friday.

I have also started the construction of the small steamship *Delavar*.

In the afternoon at school.

15. V. 1942 (Friday)

In the morning at school, in the afternoon at the ambulatory clinic and at home.

16. V. 1942 (Saturday)

It rained heavily in the morning. I went to visit Popper.

In the afternoon at home. I typed the class magazine *Outlook* on the typewriter. I'm doing it all alone and it's a lot of work.

31. Petr inserted in his diary a newspaper clipping with an article about Winston Churchill, where he underlined expressions that were characteristic of the demagogical journalism of the time. (For example: "gravedigger of the British Empire," "vulgar English suspicion," "he crowned his lies and cheating with a new arrogant lie," "he was a masterpiece of drunken madness and satanic guile," and so on).

17. V. 1942 (Sunday)

Homework in the morning. In the afternoon outside.

18. V. 1942 (Monday)

In the morning at school, in the afternoon at home.
I am redoing the map of Gross-deutsche-Reich because I was told that in the one that I had in my exercise book Moravia looked like a sausage.

19. V. 1942 (Tuesday)

In the morning at home and in town. In the afternoon at school.

20. V. 1942 (Wednesday)

In the morning at school. I had an oral test in geography and I got an A pure as milk. I deserved it for my hard labour!
In the afternoon I went for a walk with Popper.

21. V. 1942 (Thursday)

In the morning in town, in the afternoon at school.
Tomorrow and on Monday there is no school.

22. V. 1942 (Friday)

Home all day, nothing special.

23. V. 1942 (Saturday)

Nothing special.

24. V. 1942 (Sunday)
Nothing special.

25. V. 1942 (Monday)
Nothing special.

26. V. 1942 (Tuesday)
In the morning at home, in the afternoon at school.

27. V. 1942 (Wednesday)
In the morning at school. I am supposed to get a bad note from Beinkoles.
In the afternoon I went for a walk with Popper.
There was a bomb assassination attempt against SS Gruppenführer
Heydrich. That's why they ordered a state of emergency and people who will
be seen today after 9 o'clock and tomorrow before 6 o'clock and won't stop
immediately after being called will be shot dead. There is a reward of
10,000,000 crowns for whoever informs on those responsible for the assassination, and whoever knows about them and does not report it will be shot
with his entire family.

28. V. 1942 (Thursday)
This morning it was announced that Mr. Heydrich's life is not in danger.
In the afternoon at school.
In the evening they announced on loudspeakers that eight people have been
shot for sheltering unregistered persons. Among them was a seventeen-year-
old boy.

29. V. 1942 (Friday)

In the morning at school. In the afternoon at home and outside.

They are looking for someone called Valcik. Reward: 100,000 crowns.

30. V. 1942 (Saturday)

In the morning with Popper. I saw a poster about a search for yet another assassin. Reward: 10,000 crowns.

Forty-five people have been shot for publicly approving of the assassination. We dropped the magazine *Die Wehrmacht,* which Grandma has been receiving for some time for free, into the Kohners' mailbox. Mr. Kohner of course thought that Kohner sounds like an Über-German, so Germans are sending it to him for free. We'll do it again next time.

In the afternoon at home.

31. V. 1942 (Sunday)

I did my homework in the morning. In the afternoon we were all near the slaughterhouse by the rafts. There are five of them.

The reward of 10,000,000 crowns is being increased due to a contribution from the Protectorate government by another 10,000,000. The first reward came from the leader of the SS.

1. VI. 1942 (Monday)

Eighteen people have been shot, mostly for hiding unregistered persons.

In the morning at school. In the afternoon at home and outside.

In Berlin there was an attack on the Soviet Paradise exhibit and some Jews were caught nearby. So 250 [Jews] were shot and 250 deported to concentration camps.

2. VI. 1942 (Tuesday)

In the morning at home and in town, in the afternoon at school. All of Liben is closed, something was going on there, because some people in my class who are from Liben heard that someone was shot at while looking out the window. They had vehicles with German soldiers driving around there and if people (it was at about 5 o'clock) looked out the window, they shot at them. All older girls from Liben were taken away, their hair was washed, and they were let go. They are looking for some blonde who held a bicycle for the assassins.

Jews are not allowed to go to barbers.

3. VI. 1942 (Wednesday)

In the morning at school, in the afternoon with Popper.

In Berlin there was an attack on the exhibition Soviet Paradise and Jews were caught nearby. Immediately 250 [Jews] were executed, 250 [were sent] to a concentration camp.

4. VI. 1942 (Thursday)

Flags are everywhere at half-mast or black. Heydrich probably died.
That's why:

1. We were sent home early.
2. On Friday we don't have to go to school.
3. On Friday a new transport will be called up, which has to report on Sunday.

Re 1, 2: there will probably be marches and demonstrations.
In the afternoon at school.

5. VI. 1942 (Friday)

The report about SS Obergruppenführer Heydrich's death has been confirmed.

His picture in a black frame completely covers the front page of the newspapers. From 3 P.M. on Saturday until 8 A.M. on Monday Jews are not allowed to walk in Prikopy, Narodni Avenue, Wenceslas Square, and in many other places.

Rather than remember them all, I prefer to sit at home.

6. VI. 1942 (Saturday)

I went for a walk with Popper. In the afternoon at Grandma's.

7. VI. 1942 (Sunday)

I started my new book, *The Wizard from the Altay Mountains.*

My earlier novel, *Visit from Prehistory,* is now in Hradec.

The Kohners are leaving this morning. They said good-bye to all of us.

There were tears, of course. Every one of them has about 80 kg of luggage. They have to be in the exhibition grounds at 8:30.—In the afternoon at home.

8. VI. 1942 (Monday)

In the morning at school, in the afternoon at home.

9. VI. 1942 (Tuesday)

The train carrying R. Heydrich left for Berlin, where he was buried today. That's why there have to be flags at half-mast everywhere, or black ones.— Many new pupils have been accepted this afternoon, among them Harry Popper. We had a German test.

The Kohners were supposed to leave today but I don't know if they did because twelve hundred persons were called up for the transport but only a thousand left. The rest have to wait for the next one. The food at the exhibition ground is very bad.

10. VI. 1942 (Wednesday)
In the morning at school. I got an A minus on yesterday's test.
In the afternoon at home.

11. VI. 1942 (Thursday)
In the morning in town, in the afternoon at school. We had a maths test; I think I got two questions right and one wrong.

12. VI. 1942 (Friday)
Uncle Milos has been called up for Theresienstadt? Poland?
Maybe Grandma as well.
Baum (The Fatty) from our class is going.

13. VI. 1942 (Saturday)
In the morning at home, in the afternoon at Grandma's.
I heard there was a big massacre near Kladno. They found a secret transmitter and plenty of ammunition. That's why they shot all the men, women and children were taken to concentration camps, and the village (it was quite big, about a thousand houses) has been burned down. The fire could be seen from Bila Hora. When firemen came and wanted to put it out, the Germans shot at them.

14. VI. 1942 (Sunday)

In the morning I did homework; in the afternoon I went to the Miloses to say good-bye.

There is a new ditty about Jews, I'll try to get a copy of it.

Uncle Milos is going tomorrow morning.

15. VI. 1942 (Monday)

In the morning at school. A Czech grammar test. In the afternoon outside.

16. VI. 1942 (Tuesday)

In the morning at home and outside, in the afternoon at school.

17. VI. 1942 (Wednesday)

Today is the end of the deadline for the [assassin] of Reinhard Heydrich to either give himself up or be handed over. A German soldier was shot dead in Branik and two policemen were killed in Liben when they demanded someone's identity card. He reached into his pocket but instead of an identity card pulled out a gun and shot them both dead. But he was caught and he may be R. Heydrich's assassin.

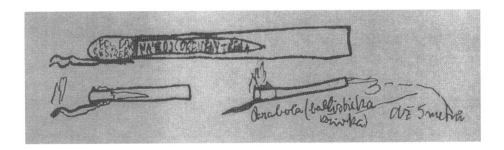

18. VI. 1942 (Thursday)

In the morning I went for a walk. I am now reading *Kondelik and Vejvara,* a book we were lent by Hanka Ginz.

In the afternoon at school. I got a D on a maths test.

I showed my cannon in class in front of an audience.

Partly as a precaution against giving away the explosive (phosphorus) before uninvited eyes, partly to fasten the fuse, I covered the glass at the end with a layer of wax.

19. VI. 1942 (Friday)

In the morning at school. I organized the third lottery draw. The first prize of 20 crowns fell to Milos Mautner, who gave it up in favor of Zinn.

In the afternoon I went for a walk.

I heard they caught the assassins in Boromejsky church. The chaplain hid them there. When Eva walked past it she heard shooting and she saw shattered windows. Again they executed 153 people.

20. VI. 1942 (Saturday)

In the morning at home. In the afternoon at Grandma's. We have to completely avoid Narodni Avenue. We walk down Truhlarska, across Hybernske (Republiky) Square, past Bambino, past the mint, we cross to the other side, where they sell suitcases, we walk past St. Havel's, Sel, across the Zelny market, past Martin in the Wall, down the police street, and through the small tunnel under Narodni Avenue.

21. VI. 1942 (Sunday)

Homework in the morning and in the afternoon. In the afternoon we also went outside.

22. VI. 1942 (Monday)

In the morning at school, in the afternoon homework.

23. VI. 1942 (Tuesday)

In the morning in town and at home, in the afternoon at school.
Czech composition: Which topics in natural history am I interested in?
I wrote: Mr. Pu's woe and bliss in the Silurian System.

24. VI. 1942 (Wednesday)

We are taught by Mr. Weislitz instead of Mr. David, who was arrested (together with his wife).—According to version No. 1 Mr. David was arrested because of talking freely, version No. 2 says his friend was arrested and informed on him that they had been in contact, and version No. 3 says that he let himself be accused so that he could go to Kolin, because his parents are currently leaving from there with a transport.

25. VI. 1942 (Thursday)

In the morning at home. In the afternoon at school.

26. VI. 1942 (Friday)

They are distributing the new transport notices.
Only Germans receive cherries. Pavel saw a woman who was holding a child and pinching its bottom. The child was crying and the woman was saying it was because he wanted strawberries, and begged that they should give her at least ¼ kg.
In the morning at school.

27. VI. 1942 (Saturday)

Our teachers Mr. Beinkoles and Miss Polakova are leaving, and Fabian. In the afternoon at Grandma's.

28. VI. 1942 (Sunday)

The Miloses were here and Eva II. Our Eva is ill, or she's at least pretending, so she won't have to go to school.

29. VI. 1942 (Monday)

Yesterday I received a summons to come today to Bet Ha'am[32] at 33 Dlouha Street. So I went there today, as our art class was cut by two hours on account of Mr. Beinkoles's departure. It has to do with support services for transports. The one leaving now is full of old people. They say the youngest man on it is fifty-four, the oldest ninety-four years old. In the afternoon I went as part of the support service to paint numbers for a Martin Heymann at 18 Balbinova Street. I received 10 crowns.

I thought I had run out of paint and I wanted to go back to Dlouha to get more, but on the way my paintbrush fell on me and messed me up nicely. This way, I realized that it still had paint in it, went back, and happily finished the job. The lady who was preparing it all for the old man said that I probably put a "broche"[33] on it. That woman laughs a lot (she is an Aryan) and the old man walks around with a hot water bottle to warm his armpits and sometimes sits in a rocking chair. He is incapable of doing anything. I was given 3 crowns for travel and a daily identity card. I've earned 10 crowns.

32. Bet Ha'am, a Jewish institution, the so-called "People's House."
33. "Blessing" in Yiddish, from Hebrew "brachah."

30. VI. 1942 (Tuesday)

I did more running around for the Hilfsdienst[34] and earned 5 crowns.

In the afternoon I was in school. I'll have all A's on my report card. Miss Lauscherova told me this so that I can tell Grandma before she leaves.

A German man threw me off the tram in a very rough manner. He said Heraus! Out! In the proper order, first in German, then in Czech, and I had to get off; he said I was carrying an unwrapped duvet.

So I had to run in terrible rain all the way to the Hilfsdienst.

1. VII. 1942 (Wednesday)

In the morning at school. In the afternoon again with the Hilfsdienst.

Grandma received the summons to a transport.

2. VII. 1942 (Thursday)

In the morning with the Hilfsdienst, and I earned 10 crowns.

3. VII. 1942 (Friday)

In the morning at school. I was stamping the report cards and of course saw them all while doing that (our class).

In the afternoon at home. I started making a gun based on phosphorus.

The idea was suggested to me by the awesome power of this explosive that recently, when I was shooting from a reloading cannon, tore the latter into pieces. My hand was bleeding in two places, Harry Popper (he was accepted into the school along with many others, because it is no longer allowed to take school exams like last year. So they will be tested like other children and re-

34. Support service

117

ceive a report card.) was also bleeding in two places, but on his neck, Traub had a cut on his forehead, and there were glass shards all over the classroom. I shot several times before from an ordinary cannon to the great amazement of all pupils, but now they are starting to be afraid of this "project" and close their eyes when it shoots.

In the afterenoon I was with the Hilfsdienst.

I won't tell Mummy about that report card; I want her to be surprised!

4. VII. 1942 (Saturday)

With the Hilfsdienst in the afternoon. I have an appointment to do some work all the way in Strasnice. I won't be able to go in the afternoon, because Saturday afternoon from 3 o'clock and all day Sunday Jews are not allowed to travel, just as they are not allowed to walk down forbidden streets. I have a weekly pass to let me go through them and I do so, but so far no one has stopped me. There were three of us in Strasnice and we were given 300 crowns, although we hardly did anything.

5. VII. 1942 (Sunday)

In the morning at home, in the afternoon outside.

6. VII. 1942 (Monday)

In the morning at school.

Grandma went to the exhibition ground at 2 o'clock. She is leaving on Thursday.

7. VII. 1942 (Tuesday)

In the morning with the Hilfsdienst.

In the afternoon they told us at school that we have no classes tomorrow. Only those who are practicing the Psalm "Nach Osten neig die Stern derb schimmern Zions reste im Abendrot "[35] should come. Unfortunately I am among them.

We were photographed. The photographer stood on the table, we sat organized on benches. The camera was a wooden box on four collapsible legs. It stood on the table, the photographer prepared the magnesium, lit it, and took a picture of us in the resulting flash. It took only 3–4 seconds.

8. VII. 1942 (Wednesday)

In the morning at school for Psalm rehearsal. In the afternoon at home.

9. VII. 1942 (Thursday)

Mummy was in Veletrh early at 5 A.M. to see Grandma board the train at Bubenec station. But soldiers were chasing her away from the street (the transport Jews walked in groups of fifty accompanied by soldiers along the southern tracks), so she ran up from the other side and saw Grandma getting into a personal carriage.

We received our report cards. Me, Hanka, and Pavel have all A's. In our class there are 40% of them (16 out of 50). We had a show; we performed a reading of the Psalm and recited poetry. One-handed Dr. Kahn visited us. But the other class (IV.C) had a nice show. Fischmann did an impression of Lauder the head

---

35. "The mighty God called the earth from the rising of the sun unto the going down thereof. Out of Zion, the perfection of beauty, God hath shined."

teacher, then of Miss Lauscherova (for this he put two hats on his breasts), and the teachers went all red, but they couldn't do anything, because it's these pupils' last year in class.

10. VII. 1942 (Friday)
In the morning at home. In the afternoon at home.

11. VII. 1942 (Saturday)
In the morning at home, in the afternoon at Aunt Anda's.

12. VII. 1942 (Sunday)
In the morning at the Hilfsdienst, in the afternoon at home.

13. VII. 1942 (Monday)
In the morning I was at the Jewish Community. I went to negotiate with Mr. Klemperer regarding tutoring his son in grammar. He wants to pay me 10 crowns per hour.
In the afternoon at the Hilfsdienst.

14. VII. 1942 (Tuesday)
In the morning outside, in the afternoon at the Hilfsdienst.

15. VII. 1942 (Wednesday)
Same. I played billiards for the first time (the kind with holes and sticks) and won 2 crowns straightaway.

16. VII. 1942 (Thursday)

Tomorrow I have to travel with the Hilfsdienst as far as Suchdol.

17. VII. 1942 (Friday)

First thing in the morning I travelled by tram and by bus to Suchdol. It's really far away. It rained all day and we had to wait at the akciz[36] for those whose suitcases we were supposed to take away. We saw an officer trying to catch a bus, but he failed and swore terribly. I laughed; the German came over to us and shouted at one of us (Hecht): Du hast gelacht?[37] The boy was expecting a slap but because he really didn't laugh (that was me), he answered quite calmly: "No." The officer then walked away.

18. VII. 1942 (Saturday)

In the morning with the Hilfsdienst, in the afternoon outdoors. I made a heavy gun out of clay and a carriage for it. Also a heavy cartridge, then a revolver, and a round bomb with an opening and a plug.

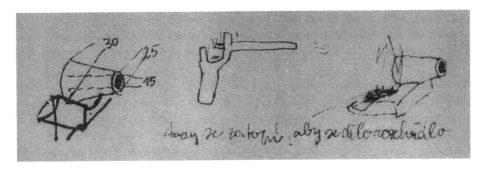

36. Akciz—tax on import of food into towns, metaphorically also the border of the taxed area.

37. "Did you laugh?"

121

19. VII. 1942 (Sunday)

In the morning at the Hilfsdienst.

Uncle Levitus and his wife are leaving with the transport. We were there in the afternoon and helped them pack. They are not worried because they had almost everything prepared.

20. VII. 1942 (Monday)

The Levituses were summoned to the transport.

21. VII. 1942 (Tuesday)

The Poppers were summoned to the transport.

22. VII. 1942 (Wednesday)

[Nothing recorded]

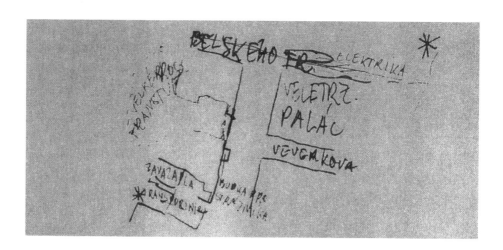

23. VII. 1942 (Thursday)

The Levituses reported to the exhibition grounds in the afternoon. I walked with them all the way to the first gate (the bottom one), where Jewish organizers were sending them to their places.

24. VII. 1942 (Friday)

In the morning at the Hilfsdienst.
The Poppers have been called off the transport. They must have bribed some gestapo man. I heard this costs 50,000 crowns for one person.

25. VII. 1942 (Saturday)

Auntie received a summons to report as an added person to transport AAv.

26. VII. 1942 (Sunday)

In the morning at home, in the afternoon with the Hilfsdienst.

27. VII. 1942 (Monday)

Auntie has left.

28. VII. 1942 (Tuesday)—1. VIII. 1942 (Saturday)

[Nothing recorded]

2. VIII. 1942 (Sunday)

There is a big removal of (postal) horses going on. There are about fifty of them on Lodecka Street. A German officer is supervising it. The place is full of their poo.

3. VIII. 1942 (Monday)

Again, they are taking dogs away to Stvanice. They are testing whether they are afraid of shooting. It is very easy to see from Hlavkuv Bridge, but policemen are chasing people away from there.

4. VIII. 1942 (Tuesday)

In the morning at home, in the afternoon outside.

5. VIII. 1942 (Wednesday)

[Nothing recorded)

6. VIII. 1942 (Thursday)

[Nothing recorded)

7. VIII. 1942 (Friday)

[Nothing recorded)

8. VIII. 1942 (Saturday)

We went to the slaughterhouse, rode on rafts, enjoyed the sun and the water, and had a good time.

9. VIII. 1942 (Sunday)

In the morning at home.

Petr Ginz (1928–1944), *Moonlit Mountain,* 1942–1944. India ink on paper; Gift of
Otto Ginz, Haifa; Collection of the Yad Vashem Art Museum, Jerusalem.

Postcard dated July 9, 1944, to Petr Ginz in Theresienstadt, from his father, Otto Ginz. From the private archives of Chava Pressburger.

DEAREST PETR,

A PACKAGE WILL BE SENT TO YOU ON JULY 12. I WILL ENCLOSE A LIST AND EXPLAIN THE ORDER IN WHICH YOU SHOULD EAT EVERYTHING. DO NOT EAT ANYTHING THAT HAS GONE BAD.

KISSES

9/7   1944

The Last Meeting
Chava Pressburger

Petr's diary accurately describes his rich life almost until the moment of his transport to Theresienstadt. He lived for two more years in Theresienstadt, during which time, in spite of difficult conditions, he continued to draw and write. He edited the magazine *Vedem*[38] and, as far as possible, lived life to the full. In two years, the naive, dreamy boy turned into a serious sixteen-year-old young man who was immensely interested in just about every scientific subject. In Theresienstadt one had the opportunity to meet acclaimed scientific experts and great artists, from many disciplines. Petr listened keenly to their lectures, which took place secretly, because any intellectual activity was strictly forbidden by the Germans.

Two years later, when I was also deported to Theresienstadt as a fourteen-year-old, I had the chance to see Petr briefly, hug him, and say good-bye to him, before he was deported with a transport to his death in Auschwitz. I wrote down the terrible moments of our last farewell in my Theresienstadt diary:

---

38. Translator's note: this can mean both "we lead" and "we are winning."

16 August 1944

Petr is an awfully smart boy. In their house he is known as the smartest. When I arrived here, a girl asked me if Petr Ginz is my brother, and said he was the most intelligent boy in the "heim." I was very happy and I was very proud of him.

16 September 1944

I haven't written for a long time, I couldn't find time to do it. Petr was ill, his fever was 39°. There is this epidemic in Theresienstadt now. Fevers, people feel no pains. I was very worried that he might have something, because Petr and I are here alone together and if something happened to him, I am responsible; how would I explain it to our parents?

27 September 1944

So Petr and Pavel are in the transport. They were summoned the day before yester-day. It was said they'd be leaving the next day, but meanwhile they are still here, be-cause the train hasn't come. They are living in the Hamburg barracks in the garret. . . . We are hoping the transport will stay here, they say there is a strike in the entire protectorate, so the train won't even get here. When I found out that Petr is in it I felt ill. I ran to the toilets and cried my heart out there.
In front of Petr I try to calm myself; I don't want to worry him. They are supposed to be taken somewhere near Dresden; I am terribly afraid there will be bombing there and the boys might get hurt. Mummy and Daddy, I miss you very much, espe-cially now that my only support will be gone. Who knows if we'll all find each other ever again? Oh, I wish the war would end already, it's already a bit too much for us! What will our parents say at home when they find out that Petr is gone? They will probably know it soon now; Karel Müller wrote it home. Poor Daddy and Mummy!

28 September 1944

The train is now here and both boys have boarded it. Petr has the number 2392 and Pavel 2626. They are together in one carriage. Petr is amazingly calm; Uncle Milos was admiring him. I kept hoping the train won't come, even though I knew the opposite was true. But what can one do?

In the morning Hanka (my cousin) and I went to see them by the slojzka.[39] It was a terrible sight, I will not forget it till I die. A throng of women, children, and old people were pushing near the barracks to get a last glimpse of their son, husband, father, or brother. The men were leaning out the windows, pushing and shoving one on top of the other, to glance their dearest. All the barracks were surrounded by police so that no one could escape. Ghetto watchmen were standing near the building and chasing away people who got too close to it. Men were waving from the windows and saying farewell with their eyes to their relatives. Crying was heard from everywhere. We quickly ran and brought the boys two slices of bread, so they won't be hungry. I pushed my way through the crowd, crawled under the rope that separated it from the barracks, and handed Petr the bread through the window. I still had time to touch his hand through the bars and already the ghetto cop chased me away. Lucky it ended there. Now the boys are gone and all we have left of them are empty beds.

12 October 1944

It has been fourteen days now since the boys left, and we haven't received any news from them. There were altogether seven transports, the list for the last one was being distributed yesterday, and I heard there will be more.

---

39. Slojzka, from the German *Schleuse*—sluice gate, was the name of the place where transports were received and sent off.

16 October 1944

Today there was an alarm again, after a long time. I saw foreign airplanes. First there were droves of them and then we saw four, followed by German fighter planes. I am terribly afraid they will bomb where our boys are. Who knows if my little Petr and I will ever meet again? Dear boy! I hope not even God could allow this to happen.

28 October 1944

Oh, today is another sad day! Uncle Milos boarded a transport to the East a moment ago. He received the summons around midnight last night, saying he has to leave at two o'clock. I heard that Günther[40] arrived here and was very angry at Rahm[41] for leaving so many Jews here. It is exactly a month today since the boys left, and now Uncle. Hanka and I will stay here all alone, the last ones from our entire family.

2 November 1944

Yesterday I found Petr's diary. When I read it, I couldn't control myself and I had to cry. Dear poor darling.

40. The chief of the anti-Jewish SS central command in Prague.

41. The last Theresienstadt Kommandant.

In Israel, one day a year is dedicated to the memory of the Holocaust. On this day, called Yom Hashoah, Holocaust Day, the media deals with this subject, documentary films are shown containing horrifying witness accounts of Holocaust survivors from different countries. A great number of these accounts were recorded many years ago, immediately after the war, when the experiences were still fresh (even though I don't believe that one can ever forget the horrors one lived through in concentration camps). Some testimonies were also used during the trial against Nazi war criminals in Nuremberg.

Israeli television broadcast a witness testimony that was extremely upsetting to me because it also had to do with the death of my brother, Petr. I heard details about how mass murder was carried out in gas chambers. I ask the readers to forgive me for returning to that terrible description. The witness in question worked in the gas chambers. His task was to wait for the people shoved into the gas chamber to suffocate; then he had to open the chamber and transport the heaps of corpses to the ovens, where they were to be burned. This man could barely speak for tears. He testified that the position of the corpses suggested what went on inside the hermetically sealed chamber, when it began to be filled with toxic gas. The stronger ones, led by an overpowering instinct for self-preservation, tried to get to the top, where there was still some air left, so that the weaker ones were trampled to death.

The picture of this horrific scene often haunts my thoughts, especially at night, even though I try to resist it. I see Petr in this terrifying situation and I find it hard to breathe myself. I ask myself: why him, and not me?

Writings from Theresienstadt

Pieces written for the magazine *Vedem* (Theresienstadt, 1942–1944)

Petr Ginz
WANDERING THROUGH THERESIENSTADT

A room buried under The Cavalier,[42] stinking of the stench of latrines, weak light, filth, physical and spiritual. The only care is to eat enough, get some sleep and . . . ? What more? A spiritual life? Could there exist anything more in those underground lairs than mere animal desire to satisfy physical needs? And still, it is possible! The seed of a creative idea does not die in mud and scum. Even there it will germinate and spread its blossom like a star shining in darkness.

The blind artist Berthold Ordner[43] is proof of this. One day I visited him with Jiricek Schubert, in order to write about him in our magazine. After a brief introduction I asked him to tell me something about himself. Unfortunately he spoke only German, so we couldn't communicate very well.

42. The so-called "home" for old prisoners.

43. Berthold Ordner, b. 1889, a Holocaust survivor, a blind Austrian artist who continued to produce unusual wire sculptures even after he was deported to Theresienstadt from Vienna.

"Ever since my youth," this man said, "I was a keen observer of everything that was happening in front of my eyes. When I was later fatally blinded, I was forced to stop drawing. I couldn't see or touch what I was drawing. I was simply missing the third dimension. And so I reached for the wire." Having said this, he took a beautiful peacock off his shelf, made of delicate copper wires. I couldn't stop admiring the beautiful lines and the detailed execution of this object. The eyes on the tail were made of wire twisted into spirals.

"And how do you work?" I asked.

"First I shape a skeleton, and if it seems to have the right shape, I work out individual details, muscles and such, using a thin wire."

"How come you still remember so exactly the shapes of models you haven't seen in over twenty-five years?"

"This is due to my memory. I use my memory to conjure up various objects that I saw in my youth, and I re-create them now, twenty years later, in the form in which I understood them back then. It is a method similar to the expressionist technique. Look at the model at home, then make it, following especially the outline and shape. Colours are secondary. It's the same with me, except the gap between observing the model and re-creating it is a little longer. Twenty-five years! So much has changed in that time! I used to have shows of my work in America, France, England, Germany, Spain, Sweden, and elsewhere; museums were fighting for my creations. Now in Theresienstadt I am starving; I don't even have enough wire to work with."

"Do you still feel your blindness?" I asked him.

"Sometimes, when I am reflecting on things, I don't feel the lack of my eyesight at all. In my spirit, I leave the dirt here completely behind. Those are my happiest moments."

Petr Ginz
LINOCUTS

As the entire linocut technique shows, a linocut is the expression of a person who does not make compromises. It is either black or white. There is no grey transition. There can't be any soaring strokes as in a painting or insane fragmented deletions, whose parallels can be found in the mad fruits of some poets' labour. Everywhere there is the same, calm line, arch, curve, plane. A sculptor, for example, cannot create his sculpture in a state of ecstasy. It would look strange if the sculptor, in a sudden attack of artistic feeling, started hitting the marble, bronze, or other material. That material would either collapse or fall apart. It is simply necessary to work calmly and over an extended period of time, during which you can instantly control the emotions that have just come up. I think that this can only help your art. Paper, music sheetnotes, and a canvass can take everything, but sculptures and linocuts cannot. So according to this I would divide art into two types, the calm and the ecstatic. Of course, this doesn't mean that every poet or writer has to create in a state of ecstasy. Not at all. Some poets write calmly, others less so. But they do have this choice. An artist working in marble does not have that choice. A linocut artist—and this applies to any engraver—does not have it either. A painter, yes, a composer, too, and so does a dancer, but not a metal craftsman. When I say, "He has a choice," you mustn't imagine that after a long deliberation he will choose one or the other. His own character chooses between calm art and art created in a state of ecstasy. And this is also how we must judge those works of art. Calm art reveals the artist's core; ecstatic art shows his mood. Picture it like this: Every day, we'll draw lines bent this way or that. These are the poet's moods. Calm art means that the poet slightly corrects every day the line from the day before, until he arrives at an average angle: this is his core. The ecstatic

Petr Ginz (1928–1944), *Night Blossoms,* 1942–1944. Linocut; 11.5 × 17 cm; Gift of Otto Ginz, Haifa; Collection of the Yad Vashem Art Museum, Jerusalem.

artist will capture one line, one mood, which may be different from the one that follows it.

But in the end I beg for your forgiveness for straying so much from the given topic. Farewell!

Petr Ginz
CRAZY AUGUST

The air was humid and chilly. Suspended in it were clusters of steely grey fog that almost touched the surface of the sea. Unpleasant light wind. A green mass of waves at a distance of about a hundred yards gradually disappeared, until it merged with the sea.

August sat in the cabin of *The Bonifacie*. They called him Crazy August, but Petr, the young sailor, believed him. "He is not mad," he used to say, "he's just different, a bit strange. He probably knows some big secret you don't and can't understand."

"You've become almost like him, you'll end up losing your marbles if you keep talking to him," the other sailors would say to him. "They are ignorant," August would say and his eyes seemed to Petr as if they were looking down at him from a high mountain, hidden by clouds. No, August was not a madman, certainly not, how could he be when he spoke so convincingly? And Petr was fond of him, he liked that crazy man with the deep eyes, he trusted him. August did speak in a strange way. "No one in the world talks like this," thought Petr. "I have never heard the captain, the ship steerer, the sailors or anyone in the port speak in such a peculiar way." For this was his entire world. It was nighttime. Everyone was asleep, only the steps of the guard with his dog could be heard on the deck. Petr was falling asleep. His muscles felt soft and relaxed.

His muscles, his entire body felt free, which also relaxed his mind. His thoughts were drifting off behind the blue fog of sleep. He was losing consciousness.

Suddenly he felt someone's light touch, like an electric spark. Petr lifted his head with difficulty in his sailor's cot, looked around, and saw the figure of Crazy August bending over him. "Come with me!" Petr sat up and stretched. "Come quickly," August's voice urged him. Petr stood up without a protest, even though it was warm under his blanket and cold outside. He followed him quietly. They entered the lower deck. August lit a candle. Its weak light barely hid the dark that was hiding behind every corner, in every crack. They reached a small room on the subdeck. Crazy August went inside and Petr followed. The key rattled in the lock and then disappeared in August's pocket. He placed the candle in the centre, sat down on a crate, and held his head in his hands. Petr crouched, as he was feeling cold. August lifted his head. His expressive face shone in the light of the candle, its small reflections dancing like tiny fires in his eyes. A moment passed. Small flies buzzed around the flame. Finally, August spoke, his voice cutting into the dead silence. "Life? What is life? It's like the light of this candle, which burns the wings of these stupid mosquitoes!" Silence again, interrupted here and there by the cracking of the candlewick. "Poor mosquitoes."—"Why do they fly so much around this light?"—Pause. Slowly, he spoke to himself, as if reflecting: "Habit—a move toward individual existence and uncertainty . . . " He buried his head again in his hands and said harshly: "They fly, fascinated, around the flame, until it burns them and they fall down, destroyed. Idiots!"—"Idiots? Habit and uncertainty are too strong, they can't overcome them. Poor insects! . . . " They both sat in silence. Petr was actually surprised—how come he was there instead of sleeping peacefully in his cot? "Think about life, my boy," August said to him, "look, it is like this flame. Do you see it, do you understand it? We circle it out of habit, and we must die. We want to be ourselves, and we sacrifice everything for this price!"

He reached out and extinguished the candle. Darkness enveloped the room. The mosquitoes could be heard flying away, deprived of the fascinating candle flame. They whizzed around for a little while longer, but soon the buzzing of their wings stopped. They probably made their way into the open space through some crack.

"Did you see, did you see?" August's voice spoke from the dark. "Did you pay good attention, my boy?" he repeated as he removed the lid of the crate with gunpowder.

"One more time, Flamarion." The captain could be heard as if from a far distance, playing cards.

"Deliverance . . . " August whispered. He straightened his hand and threw a lit match flame into the crate of powder.

And the room was lit up by a tremendous glow, and in the blaze of the explosion Petr saw the light of the Great Communion.

Petr Ginz
THE ORCHIDS THIEF

Once upon a time there was a gardener who took great pride in his horticultural talents. His special hobby was orchids. He was especially dedicated to one flower bed. He fertilized it carefully with potassium chlorate, watered and nurtured it. He also had a few more patches of orchids that he was not so concerned about. He left them to nature and birds and wasn't at all surprised when these orchids began to rot, the flowers were not that big, beautiful and heavy. What used to look like orchids turned into quite ugly little monsters, creepy and disgusting. But the nurtured orchids were blossoming, they were becoming more and more beautiful and the gardener couldn't stop looking at them. "When I sell them," he said to himself, "I will be well off until the end of my life, because no one in the world has such beautiful orchids." Every Tuesday, rich men from town would come to buy flowers. The gardener was looking forward to their arrival, although he was sorry to be selling the beautiful orchids.

On Monday night the gardener suddenly heard quiet footsteps squeaking on the sand in the garden. "Such a late buyer?" he wondered and looked out the window. And what does he see? A ragged boy carrying a basket is quickly approaching the flower bed with the beautiful orchids. He looks around to see if he is being observed, then bends down and quickly begins to pluck the beautiful flowers. When the boy stood crying in the gardener's shed, without the basket, without the orchids, the gardener said: "Why did you want to steal my orchids? Didn't you feel sorry for them?" The boy remains wilfully silent. He is standing in the light of the kerosene lamp and his face looks white, twisted, his sleeves are like the leaves, the haggard body like the stem of—those uncared-for orchids! And that silence of his! Everything is as if intentionally arranged so that I will understand!

The gardener realized the truth; he saw that the boy was the product of a ruined and bad world, just like the neglected flowers had become deformed through his own mistreatment of them. Was that a reason to punish the boy? It would be the same as punishing neglected orchids for being ugly. In the meantime, the boy disappeared. "Really, these orchids are basically the same, but the environment caused good qualities to develop on one side, bad ones on the other. Yes, and this is called character in people, a collection of tendencies. Under the influence of the environment, these tendencies are either

140

blocked, or developed. And it is the task of gardeners in the entire world to take good care of and to water the gardens that have been entrusted to them."

Thus the gardener sat long into the night and reflected, until he fell asleep, his head on his chest. Sleep well, gardener, and may you dream about a garden full of beautiful white orchids.

Petr Ginz
EXCERPT FROM THE UNFINISHED NOVEL
THE SECRET OF SATAN'S GROTTO

. . . An adult usually pretends that he thinks only about sensible and worthy things, but this isn't true. In unguarded moments when the ironclad vest surrounding his head opens up and his real face appears, the mask of social stiffness falls off. And I think he feels better when this happens. I know it from my own experience: having once lost my way in the woods and found a lake with dark, calm water, I threw a pebble into it and was very happy to see the circles spreading fast.

It occurred to me then that my feelings at that moment were like a newspaper before it hits the rolling press. All the pressure from every side disappeared. I wondered: why does the pure paper of children's souls have to pass from a young age through the rolling press of life and society, which imprints it with all sorts of qualities and crushes it under the pressure of worries about livelihood and the attacks of enemies. Just as the paper thinks that the picture of its life has been printed, it reenters the printing machine, which prints more qualities and opinions on top of the others, often not complementing but rather contradicting them. Every colour tries to take up as much space as possible on the paper, then a new one comes and can replace the old one. And it's sad that the paper can't change it any longer, it is moved back and forth and covered with print without any regard for its own will, and when the rotating press finally spits out the finished copy and sends it off into the world, it enters a battle against other printed copies, which were maybe accidentally produced differently.

The world is a rumpus, if you look at it objectively . . .

Notes to Petr Ginz's Diaries

(in chronological order, corresponding to the entries)
Chava Pressburger

19. IX. 1941

Jews were told to wear a badge . . . Police ordinance of 1 September 1942 forced Jews to wear a yellow six-cornered star in public with the black inscription Jude. This separation of Jews from the rest of society was the first step by the Nazis toward "the final solution of the Jewish question." K. H. Frank, Protector of Bohemia and Moravia, asked the Reichskanzlei for permission to mark the Jews in order to separate them from the rest of Czech citizens. After several cases of expressions of solidarity by Czechs (workers in a Moravian chocolate factory came to work wearing yellow stars), it was announced that whoever is seen with Jews or publicly declares that he sympathizes with them will be treated as a Jew. He will receive limited food rations, no tobacco or clothes rations, and will have to wear a yellow star himself.

In the afternoon I went with Eva to Troja . . . A suburb of Prague that Jews were allowed to frequent. Jews were forbidden to go in the opposite direction, against the flow of the Vltava River, along the embankment in the direction of the Old Town.

22. IX. 1941

. . . near the slaughterhouse . . . Prague central slaughterhouse in Holesovice (opened in 1895, finally closed down in 1983), today Prague Market Place (Trznice).

25. IX. 1941

Denis train station . . . The Ginz family lived on Starkova Street in Tesnov (called Starek-Gasse during German occupation), directly opposite the Denis station, which was called Vltavske during the war (Moldau-Bahnhof). The station building was torn down in 1972.

27. IX. 1941

Signed by Heydrich instead of Neurath . . . Konstantin von Neurath, Nazi politician and diplomat, was from 1939 Reich Protector of Bohemia and Moravia. After the war he was sentenced by the Nuremberg tribunal as a war criminal. On September 29, 1941, Neurath left for a "health vacation" and the new Reich Protector in the Czech and Moravian Protectorate became SS Obergruppenführer and police general Reinhard Heydrich, chief of the central office of Reich security (RSHA). He instantly introduced harsh repressive measures and declared a state of emergency, during which by January 1 about six hundred persons were executed. K. H. Frank was named as his successor.

6. X. 1941

There is a new inventory . . . Jewish possessions were gradually listed, cataloged, and confiscated.

10. X. 1941

Ehrlich . . . is leaving with the first transport . . . On October 16, 1942, the first transport of Prague Jews left for the ghetto in Lodz, Poland. This is the be-

144

ginning of a new phase in the persecution of Jews, which began in Germany in 1933, when Hitler was elected chancellor of the German Reich. The second phase occurred in 1935 with the publication of the Nuremberg race laws, where Jews were defined as a lower race and deprived of all civil rights.

This new phase in fact begins with a long meeting between Hitler and Himmler in September 1941, after which Himmler wrote to his closest colleagues: The Führer wishes that Germany and the Protectorate be as soon as possible emptied and freed of Jews. Most of the first transport to Lodz, which consisted of a thousand people, was murdered immediately upon arrival and only a few individuals survived.

13. X. 1941

I received notice to go to school and fill sacks with sawdust. . . . The full sacks are sent to Veletrzni Palace . . . Famous building of Czech constructivist period, a palace built in Prague 7, Holesovice, during the years 1925–1928 for the purpose of presenting Prague trade fairs and exhibitions. From 1939 the palace and its adjoining grounds were used by German Reich authorities for assembling Jews before the departure to concentration camps. The Germans convinced Jewish authorities everywhere in Europe that it was in their own interest to co-operate so as to make the resettlement of Jews as smooth as possible, stressing that it would be made more painless. The Jewish community and its leadership were fully involved in these efforts. Children filled sacks on which those who were called up for transports slept while waiting. The Prague Jewish Community had twenty times more employees than in peace times. Every Jew knew that bad things were happening, but no one guessed what a cruel fate was in store for all of them.

Between 16. X. 1941 and 3. XI. 1941

Six transports left for Lodz and one for Riga. Petr remembers the departure of relatives, the Miluskas and the Jirinas. The registration activity is intensified, organized by the Jewish Community under Nazi supervision. The elimination of the Jewish population is gathering speed.

3. XI. 1941

To Regnartova Street . . . Jachymova Street, Old Town (Josefov), was named during the years 1940–1945 after Jakob Regnart, a composer and musician at the court of Rudolf II.

23. XI. 1941

Transports to Poland . . . are stopped for the time being; now they are sending people to work in Theresienstadt . . . The town of Terezin (Theresienstadt), sixty-five kilometers north of Prague, former fortress built during the reign of Josef II in the years 1780–1790. The first transport arrived here on November 24, 1942. By the order of the Reich Protector of February 16, 1942, Theresienstadt was declared a closed Jewish settlement, a concentration camp. Altogether 140,000 prisoners passed through it.

In November 1941 the Nazis came to the conclusion that they had insufficient means for exterminating so many Jews in a short period of time and therefore, in order to prevent Jews from continuing to live among Aryans, it was decided to concentrate them in temporary ghettos. Only later did the construction and improvement of gas chambers and crematoria allow them to commit mass murder at full speed. Therefore, they asked the president of the Jewish religious community, Dr. Weidemann, and his deputy to work together and present proposals for the creation of ghettos. Their promise that transports to Poland would be stopped quickly spread among the Jewish population. The

Germans did not keep their word and on November 26, 1941, another transport left for Poland.

The lie was the foundation of all relations of Germans toward the Jews. After his conversation with Eichmann, the deputy president of the Jewish Community, Jakub Edelstein, was convinced that the creation of the ghetto could save many Czech Jews. Edelstein even demanded that young and strong Jews volunteer to go, in order to prepare an adequate basis for a self-governing Jewish town with bearable living conditions. He decided to leave for Theresienstadt himself and on December 4, 1941, he travelled there with his Prague team, by a regular personal train and carrying only a small suitcase. He thought that he could return for the rest of his luggage later. But he quickly realized that he had been lied to.

Here are two examples from an infinite number of the Nazis' lies:

When the Theresienstadt SS caught two letters that had been sent illegally, they assembled the entire population of the ghetto and the Kommandant, Dr. Seidl, announced that if those who had written them come forward, nothing will happen to them. But if they don't, there will be terrible repercussions. After a brief hesitation two seventeen-year-olds came forward; they had written to relatives, one of them to his grandmother. Both were arrested. The next day all the prisoners were assembled again and the two boys were publicly hanged.

In the small town of Horodenko in the Ukraine the Nazis ordered all Jews to report to the local church for vaccination against typhoid. Twenty-five hundred people were assembled there. They were loaded into trucks and driven to the bank of the river Dnester. When they arrived there, there was an orchestra playing and German officers were sitting at tables laden with food and drink. Large pits had been dug out opposite the officers. Between the pits and the tables lay soldiers with machine guns. When the Jews arrived, they had to stand next to the pits and were shot at in such a way as to fall directly into them. At night, a small number of Jews who were not mortally wounded ran away and told about what had happened there. A Sonderkommando arrived in the morning and pulled out the dead Jews' gold teeth. Even those who were still moving were covered with earth.

For the sake of truth it must be added that one of the German officers, Fiedler, who was responsible for auxiliary labor and commanded a group of Jewish prisoners, was always decent to them. He also tried to warn them that the "vaccination" action was a trap.

2. XII. 1941

opened by Deputy Mayor Klapka . . . From March 15, 1939, the Prague city hall was gradually becoming an organ of the Reich occupation powers. It was led by J. Pfitzner, professor of history at Prague German University, whose authority grew with the escalation of the German oppression. The last mayor, Dr. Otokar Klapka (born 1891), was shot by the Nazis on October 4, 1941.

8. XII. 1941

Japan has officially declared . . . On December 7, 1941, Japanese bombers attacked the American military base Pearl Harbor in the Hawaiian islands. The next day President Roosevelt declared war against Japan.

9. XII. 1941

The Japanese attacked . . . On December 8, 1941, after attacking American and British holdings in the Pacific Ocean, the Japanese army occupied Thailand and quickly moved south through British Malaysia in the direction of Singapore. They arrived in the domain of Singapore on December 29, 1941, and conquered the city itself on February 15, 1942.

11. XII. 1941

Stefanik's Bridge . . .   The chain bridge from the year 1868 was originally named after Franz Josef I; from 1918 it was called Stefanik's Bridge, during the years 1941–1945 Janacek's Bridge. After the war, in 1947, it was taken apart and in 1951 a new one made of concrete, called Sverma's Bridge, was built in its place.

12. XII. 1941

On the way I saw six moving vans . . . about twenty Jews (among them Uncle Milos) were carrying furniture . . . German fascism did not mean only mass murder. It was murder that went hand in hand with the biggest looting in the history of mankind. It has been estimated that the theft of Jewish property during the Protectorate reached at least 2 billion Deutsch marks, i.e., at least 20 billion Protectorate crowns. On February 12, 1941, the Reich Protector published a decree forcing Jewish businesses to declare all home and foreign working capital. These confiscated items were transferred to the Evacuation Fund of the Central Committee for Jewish expulsion. Jews had to give up land, stock shares, bank accounts, securities, jewellery, and so on. The Gestapo enforced the fulfilling of these orders by applying drastic measures in businesses and households, with the co-operation of German occupation authorities and the Protectorate police force, often on the basis of a denunciation by a German or Czech fascist.

But the Evacuation Fund did not include the enormous value of possessions the departing Jews were forced to leave behind in their homes. A special organization was set up for clearing them out, a so-called Treuhandstelle. By October 1, 1940, 14,920 Jewish apartments were registered in Prague. From the first 2,101 apartments, the furniture alone was estimated to be worth 25 million and stored in storage rooms of 36,400 square meters. The next storage area required a space of 145,600 square meters, three and a half times bigger than the Wenceslas Square in Prague. The Treuhandstelle document stated that by this date the looted collection consisted of almost 2.9 million textiles and the same amount of kitchen and household tools, more than a million pieces of porcelain and glass, more than 61,000 electrical items, almost 9,000 technical and optical instruments, more than 3,200 sewing machines, 2,500 bicycles, 34,500 fur coats, 52,000 rugs, 144,000 paintings, 1.2 million tons of coal and firewood, etc. (Miroslav Karny, *The Final Solution*).

The last theft took place upon the Jews' arrival in extermination camps, where their personal luggage was taken away from them and their gold teeth pulled out after their death.

18. XII. 1941
new crown coins . . . The Germans introduced a forced, non-real currency value against the mark. The new, Protectorate crown, displayed the armorial lion and on the reverse side the leaves of a linden tree. It was valid during 1941–1944.

22. XII. 1941
Hitler is not doing well in Russia . . . On September 21, 1941, Hitler took over the high command of the ground forces.

1. I. 1942
Jews don't have fruit . . . Already in October 1939, a system of rations for food and other consumer items was introduced in the Protectorate of Bohemia and Moravia, which seriously disadvantaged Jewish citizens. In the course of the war years these rations were increasingly restricted, which lowered especially the living standards of the urban population.

150

20. I. 1942

A new government . . . on January 19, 1942, R. Heydrich canceled the "civilian state of emergency" and simultaneously named a new Protectorate government led by Dr J. Krejci. E. Moravec was appointed as minister of education. He was an infamous publicist and demagogue who constantly appealed to his fellow citizens to loyally embrace Nazi Germany.

22. I. 1942

There are new transports to Theresienstadt . . . On January 20, 1942, a well-known conference took place in Wannsee about the final solution of the Jewish question. This is not where it was decided to exterminate all the Jews —this had been Hitler's plan since 1939. The discussion was about the best strategy to achieve this goal. The conference was organized by Heydrich and the participants were the highest functionaries involved in the elimination of Jews. Among other things, it was reported that a special Einsatzkommando will be deployed in Russia, which will shoot Jews immediately after conquering new areas. More gas chambers were to be introduced and their size increased.

Eichmann gave a detailed report about Theresienstadt. The lies about this place had to differ. For example, in Germany it had to be described as a ghetto for old people "to keep up the pretense" for the outside world. Theresienstadt was to fulfill three functions:

1. A concentration and transition camp on the way to extermination camps in Poland.
2. An instrument for the destruction of prisoners.
3. Disinformation about the fate of the Jewish population.

This last function is well illustrated by events in Theresienstadt, when the ghetto was preparing for the visit of the Red Cross commission on June 23, 1944. For this purpose, certain parts of the town along the visitors' planned route were made to look nice. Children's playgrounds were quickly set up, people sat in cafés drinking coffee, young swimmers were swimming in the river Ohre, the prisoners' food that day was of specially good quality, and many other similarly deceptive details. The commission later reported in Switzerland how comfortable the Jews are in Theresienstadt. They happily allowed themselves to be cheated by the Nazis and made no independent effort to find out about the real life of Theresienstadt inmates.

The Red Cross delegation arrived without the main officials who had demanded the visit (the president of the Red Cross, the Swedish and Danish ambassadors), but was represented only by the vice president the of Red Cross in Berlin, Dr. Rossel. He wrote a report about a wonderful, completely normal Jewish town, where people live happily and without worries. And he had written this in spite of the fact that the Red Cross had precise information about what was going on and the Theresienstadt camouflage was obvious. At that time, they already had in Geneva the authentic testimony of two inmates who had escaped from Auschwitz, Rudolf Vrba and Alfred Wetzler. The scenes that Dr. Rossel had photographed in Theresienstadt were given to the German Ministry of Propaganda for their use.

26. II. 1942

There was a bomb assassination . . . Franz von Papen (1879–1969), Nazi politician, in the years 1939–1944 active as a diplomat in Turkey.

5. IV. 1942

The apartment was locked and covered with stickers . . . "Treuhandstelle" was a department set up by the Jewish religious community in Prague according to a decree of October 13, 1941, to take over and be in charge ("treuhänderisch verwalten") of furniture and other possessions of evacuees and people transported to concentration camps. It also had a list of abandoned apartments.

20. IV. 1942

Hitler is fifty-three years old . . . On Hitler's birthday, on April 20, 1942, R. Heydrich received in a festively decorated Hlavni (Main) train station a completely equipped ambulance train as a gift from President Emil Hacha to Adolf Hitler.

27. V. 1942

There was an assassination attempt . . . R. Heydrich was mortally wounded during an assassination attempt carried out by a group of paratroopers from a Czech resistance unit based in England. The Nazis, led by the new Protector Kurt Daluege and K. H. Frank, responded to Heydrich's death with a terrible persecution of the population. In Prague alone, by July 3, 1942, 442 persons were executed without a reason.

19. VI. 1942

they caught the assassins . . . On June 18, 1942, someone betrayed the group of paratroopers hiding in Karel Boromejsky's church on Resslova Street in Prague, not far from Karlovo Square. Seven paratroopers were hidden there by Chaplain Petrek. Among them were both organizers of the assassination, Jan Kubis and Jozef Gabcik, also Josef Valcik, Adolf Opalka, and others. After a hopeless battle the heavily wounded paratroopers took their own lives. With the action on Resslova Street, the emergency law and punitive measures did not end—on the contrary, arrests and executions continued: the next day, the Czech prime minister, General Alois Elias, was executed; on June 24, 1942, the Nazis levelled the settlement Lezaky near Louka (Chrudim area), whose adult population was shot to death. Of thirteen children only two returned after the war.

1. VII. 1942

Grandma received the summons to a transport. . . . Within a single month from July 9, to August 10, 1942, Theresienstadt received altogether eight transports from Prague, bringing an influx of 8,460 Jews.

28. VII. 1942—1. VIII. 1942

no entries

5. VIII. 1942—7. VIII. 42

nothing written

The diary ends two months before the day when Petr himself joined a transport, on October 22, 1942.

Earlier, he records that Uncle Milos leaves with his transport on June 14, on June 27 three teachers from his school, on July 1 his grandmother, on July 23 Father's sister Herma and her husband Levitus, on July 28 Aunt Anda. So it seems that the Germans decided that the conditions were ripe for the total annihilation of Jewish Prague. Within a few months they deported more than twenty thousand people from Prague.

154

Toward the end of his diary Petr's handwriting becomes nervous; his writing is different, disorganized, unsteady. It is clear that he is going through a major psychological crisis; he feels that it is now his own turn.

His childhood has ended; the happy life with his parents, his sister, his school is finished. Fourteen-year-old Petr begins two years of living in Theresienstadt with new friends and new creative projects. Two years, which end with his journey to a gas chamber in Poland.

Acknowledgments
Chava Pressburger

I thank
especially my husband Avram
for his tireless support of my efforts to publish the diary
and my children Tami and Yoram,

the Yad Vashem Museum in Jerusalem for moral and financial help,

the Israeli Embassy in Prague.
H.E. Ambassador Mr. Arthur Avnon
and Secretary Mr. Valid Abu Haya
for their help in acquiring Petr's bequest,

Dr. Leo Pavlat, Director of the Jewish Museum in Prague,
for the introduction he wrote for the original Czech edition

Vladislav Zadrobilek and his daughters
Karolina and Zuzana of Trigon Publishing House
for their personal attention and professional production of this book,
my dear friends Mr. Jiri Kotouc
and Mr. Stanislav Motl for their help and advice,

and Mr. Jiri Ruzicka from Ricany,
who found and preserved Petr's diaries.

The Fates of Those in Petr's Diary*

Jewish Relatives and Friends

Ginz, Petr	died at Auschwitz in 1944
Ginz, Pavel	died at Dachau in 1944
Ginz(ova), Berta (grandmother)	died at Theresienstadt in 1943
Ginz, Emil (uncle Milos),	sent to Auschwitz in 1944. Did not return.
Ginz, Victor (uncle Slava)	died at Auschwitz in 1943
Ginz(ova), Herma (auntie Herma Levitus)	died at Maly Trostinec in 1942
Ginz(ova), Anna (auntie Anda,	died at Auschwitz in 1943

Petr's father, Otto Ginz, Petr's sister, Eva Ginz (now Chava Pressburger), and Petr's cousin Hana Ginz (now Hana Skorpilova) survived.

Other Nearest Relatives

Levitus, Karel (uncle)	died at Maly Trostinec in 1942
The Hanzl family: Pavlicek, Jozka, Jirina, Miluska	died at Lodz in 1941

Neighbors

Kohner, Lianka, and her parents	Deported to Thesesienstadt in 1942. Did not return.
Mautner family (Ervin, Karel, Egon)	Deported to Thesesienstadt in 1942. Did not return.

Petr's Friends and Schoolmates

Popper, Harry	died at Treblinka in 1942
Ehrlich, Richard	died at Lodz in 1941
Kaufmann, Heinz	died at Lodz in 1941
Hayek, Zdenek	died at Lodz in 1941
Stein, Slavek	died at Dachau
Klein, Tomas	died at Auschwitz in 1943
Hirsch(ova), Renata	died at Zamosc in 1942
Bardach, Felix	died at Zamosc in 1942
Baer(ova), Gertruda	died at Sobibor in 1942
Goldmann(ova), Rita	died at Izbica in 1942
Zinn, Erich	died at Treblinka
Stern, Hanus	died at Zamosc
Baum, Hanus	died at Auschwitz in 1944
Dusner, Ivan	died at Sobibor, Ossova in 1942
Fischhoff(ova), Edita	died at Auschwitz in 1944

Wolfgang Adler survived Auschwitz and was liberated at Gunskirchen

Teachers at the Jewish School

Glanzberg, Jiri	died in Auschwitz or Treblinka
Stein, Elisa	died in Auschwitz or Treblinka
David, Robert	died in Auschwitz or Treblinka
Weislitz (Ervin?, Josef?,Vitezslav?)	died in Auschwitz or Treblinka
Beinkoles, Jan	died at Auschwitz in 1943

Irma Lauscher(ova) survived and was liberated at Theresienstadt

Others

Bondy, Emil	deported to Theresienstadt in 1941. Died in Riga in 1942.
Kolben, Emil	died at Theresienstadt in 1943
Dr. Reich, Karel	unknown
Heymann, Martin	died at Theresienstadt
Dr. Storzova, Anne	died at Maly Trostinec in 1942.

Hanka Steinerova survived and was liberated from Auschwitz

*This is not a comprehensive list. The fate of several people Petr mentioned remains unknown.

Drawings

Deník

Petra Ginze

od devatenáctého září roku
dvacátého čtyřicátého prvého
(pátek)

do dvacátého třetího února roku
devatenáctistého čtyřicátého druhého
(pondělí)

Materiál darem Evy Ginzové
k narozeninám.

Title page of the first diary

19.IX.1941. (Pátek)

Počasí je (pě) mlhavé.

Byl zaveden odznak pro
Židy, který je asi takový:

Když jsem šel do školy, na-
počítal jsem 69 „šerifů"; ma-
minka pak jich napočítala
přes sto. Dlouhá třída je na-
zvána „Mléčnou dráhou".

Odpoledne jsem šel s Evou (lodi.
do Troje a vozili jsme na uvázané

Page from the first diary

Potom jsem chtěl mamince ulít z olova monogram, ale nepovedl se mi. Udělal jsem si pozitivní ryt do linolea, ten jsem položil na dno křížové bedničky a do té jsem nalil olovo.

Vlak měl přijet ve ¼ na 8, ale zpožděním přijel až ve ¾ 8. Manči byla celá zničená, spolucestující byli samí lupiči a zločinci.

Manči přivezla spoustu cukroví, pečiva a p.. Husa, kterou též M. přivezla vážl 6·60.

Dostal jsem jako dárek od tetičky Božky flanelovou košili, Eva bačkorky.

Hitlerovi se to na Rusku nevede a proto odstranil generála a sám šel na jeho místo.

Úterý 23. XII. 1941

Právě jsme dostali oznámení od židovské obce, abychom odevzdali do 31. prosince foukací harmoniky, a jiné hud. nástroje. teploměry a p., fotoaparáty a ...

Mimo to se musí přihlásit neprá... nožní hud. nástroje.

Page from the first diary

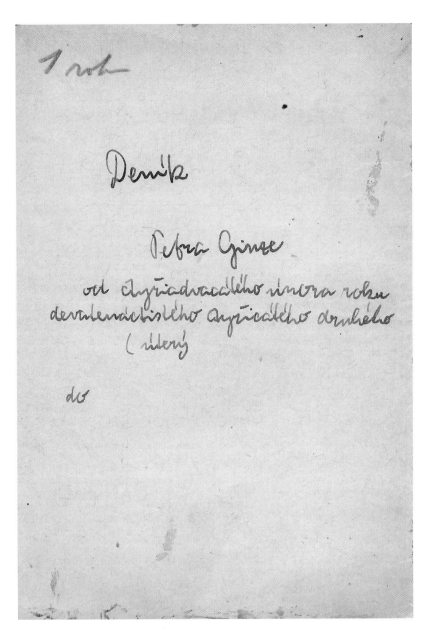

Deník

Petra Ginze
od dvacadvacátého unora roku
devatenáctistého dvacátého druhého
(úterý

do

Title page of the second diary

japonských měst.

Dopoledne doma, odpoledne zde
byli Milošovia babička.

Pondělí 20. IV. 42

V 6 h ráno odjel strýček Sláva
a Miloš do Mořiny poblíže Karlštejna
(ne Křivoklátu). Dopoledne doma a ve
městě,* odpoledne též.

Hitlerovi je 53 let, všude
prapory a průvody a v každé vý-
kladní skříni je jeho busta. Kaž-
dý dům musel vyvěsit prapor s
Hakenkreuzem, ačkoli Židům ne-
dostane se toho potěšení. Jest jim
to přísně zakázáno. Odpoledne s
tatínkem na Smíchově. Pak jsme se
se jel rozloučit s p. Felixem Ledererem
z Petrského nábřeží. Odjíždí zítra
ráno do Terezína. — Též Friedländro-
vi mají jet, ačkoli se p. Friedländr

* před Masvinm Wilsonovym) nádraží

Úterý 2. V. 42

Dopoledne doma a ve městě odpoledne ve škole. Celá Libeň byla uzavřena. Něco se tam dělo, neboť někteří zařibné z naší třídy slyšeli, jak byl někdo zastřelen, jak se dívali, jezdily tam tudy vozy s německými vojáky a když se někdo (bylo to asi v 1/2 h) díval z okna, tak po něm bouchli lidé ne... smějí se holičem.

Středa 3. V. 42

Dopoledne ve škole. Odpoledne venku. V Berlíně byl nějaký atentát na nastavu, v sovětský rádu a v okolosti bylo postříleno mnoho lidí. Zemřel prý o 250 popraveno, 250 do koncentráku.

Všechny starší dívky z Libně byly odvedeny, vypravuí jsem vlamy a zase propuštěny...

Hodili jsme Kolnerovi do schránky časopis Die Wehrmacht, který dostává bezvírka již delší čas zdarma. Člen u. myslí ovšem, že samozřejmě, přece Kolner, to je č. 44. Jistě nějaký Volksgerman, takže mu to Němci zdarma posílají.

Petr Ginz (1928–1944), *Sunflower,* 1944. Watercolour on paper, 14.5 × 21 cm; Gift of Otto Ginz, Haifa; Collection of the Yad Vashem Art Museum, Jerusalem.

Petr Ginz (1928–1944), *Flowers,* 1944. Watercolour on paper. From the private collection of Chava Pressburger.

Petr Ginz (1928–1944), *Flowers,* 1944. Watercolour on paper. From the private collection of Chava Pressburger.

Petr Ginz (1928–1944), *Rooftops and Towers of Prague,* 1939–1940(?). Watercolour and India ink on paper, 19 × 12.5 cm; Gift of Otto Ginz, Haifa; Collection of the Yad Vashem Art Museum, Jerusalem.

Petr Ginz (1928–1944), *Courtyard,* 1942–1944. Pencil on paper, 21 × 28.5 cm; Gift of Otto Ginz, Haifa; Collection of the Yad Vashem Museum, Jerusalem.

(Ghetto drawing) Theresienstadt: Petr Ginz, Illustration, 1943. From the private collection of Petr's sister, Chava Pressburger, Israel.

Petr Ginz (1928–1944), *Youth Barrack's Dwellings,* 1943. Watercolour on paper, 29.5 × 21 cm; Gift of Otto Ginz, Haifa; Collection of the Yad Vashem Art Museum, Jerusalem.

Petr Ginz (1928–1944) *Theresienstadt Dwellings,* 1942–1944. Watercolour on paper, 21 ×
14.5 cm; donation of Otto Ginz, Haifa. Collection of Yad Vashem Art Museum, Jerusalem.

Petr Ginz (1928–1944), *Ghetto Dwellings,* 1943. Watercolour on paper, 30 × 22 cm; Gift of Otto Ginz, Haifa; Collection of the Yad Vashem Art Museum, Jerusalem.

31 **Kč**

MĚSÍČNÍ KRAJINA
TEREZÍN
1942-1944

PETR GINZ
[1928-1944]

ČESKÁ REPUBLIKA

COLUMBIA STS 107

KRESBA PETRA GINZE JE V MAJETKU
YAD VASHEM ART MUSEUM
JERUZALÉM

Postal stamp published on the occasion of the explosion of the U.S. space shuttle *Columbia* STS 107, when Israeli astronaut Ilan Ramon perished with the others. He had taken a reproduction of this drawing with him into space. The graphic design is by the artist and designer Pavel Hrach. The engravings are by Vaclav Fajt.